Maureen –
Sending abundant
Creation blessings
your way —

Gia
2014

Nature's Success System

Secrets to Energize Your Health, Wealth, and Passion with the Feminine Power of Creation

Lisa Michaels, Leslie Clayton, Chantal Debrosse, Claudia Harsh MD, Tammy Huber-Wilkins MD, Judy Keating MA, Helen Magers LPCC, Mackey McNeill CPA, Paula York

Institute of Conscious Expression Company
Atlanta, Georgia

BALBOA.
PRESS
A DIVISION OF HAY HOUSE

Balboa Press books may be ordered through booksellers or by contacting:

Balboa Press
A Division of Hay House
1663 Liberty Drive
Bloomington, IN 47403
www.balboapress.com
1-(877) 407-4847

ISBN: 978-1-4525-3751-1 (sc)
ISBN: 978-1-4525-3750-4 (e)

Library of Congress Control Number: 2011914399

Printed in the United States of America

Balboa Press rev. date: 08/24/2011

"The riches of Mother Earth provide a powerful model for creating success in every area of life. These Natural Rhythms experts show you how to apply it to everything from wealth to health. You owe it to yourself to discover how to apply her rhythmic growing principles to boost your ability to thrive."
~ Sharon Lechter, CEO of Pay Your Family First and Co-Author of *Outwitting the Devil*

"Nature's Success System inspires you to a new way of walking in the world, one filled with grace and ease and in concert with Mother Nature herself. Explore, learn and tap into the wisdom."
~ Jennifer Read Hawthorne, speaker, editor, and co-author of the #1 NY Times bestseller *Chicken Soup for the Woman's Soul* and *Life Lessons for Loving the Way You Live*

"From the moment I meet Lisa Michaels her connection to the rhythms of nature was an obviously cellular knowing that far surpasses the awareness of the rest of us. Her writings are a gift to any of us who want to understand, and be at home in our skin, and our own nature in a way we never knew possible. This book by Lisa and her companions on this journey is a gift to all of us who long for that connection which she makes not only possible but easily achievable."
~ Dr. Dorothy A. Martin-Neville

"A must read! Lisa and her Natural Rhythm experts share their transformational secrets to igniting your feminine powers of creation and inspire you to align with Nature to create more health, wealth, passion, and happiness."
~ Linda Joy, Publisher of Aspire Magazine

"This book is nothing short of an evening around the fire with the ancient grandmothers who, lovingly share Nature's road map to being fully alive."
~ Michael Trotta, MPS, Founder & Executive Director, Sagefire Institute for Natural Coaching

"When women apply Nature's power of creation in their lives it connects them to their deep feminine essence. We need this level of women's wisdom in the world today."
~ Kris Steinnes, Author and Founder, Women of Wisdom Foundation

"Women leading their lives from a connection to the natural world creates an environment where masculine and feminine energy resides in sacred balance and harmony. This book provides profound tools to support your ability to thrive in alignment with your feminine essence."
~ Colin Tipping Author of *Radical Forgiveness*

"If you're looking for a spiritual, self-help book, thoroughly entertaining, which plays between a beautiful lyricism and a pinpoint practicality, this is it. Written for women, this book is a thoroughly satisfying read and contains everything we want to experience in a great book."
~ Martha Burgess, President, Martha Burgess Performance Training

"I am thrilled to see that this book is going to reach a large audience and invite more men and women to discover Nature as a path for moving from merely surviving into THRIVING. This book shares a unique Elemental approach to viewing your self and the issues that you face. There are many wonderful stories points of view and exercises from many different healers who share Nature as a healing language. This book invites you to step out into Nature and step into your greatest self."
~ Sarah Bamford Seidelmann Author, MD followyourfeelgood.com

"Natural Rhythms expert, Dr. Huber-Wilkins has found a way to blend traditional psychiatry with the energy work of Natural Rhythms. Through this work I've learned to ground myself in the energy of mother earth, to set intentions with the help of angels, to be cleansed with the healing nature of water, to live with the passionate power of fire, and to believe in the essence of spirit."
~ Lori Plogsted

"My intention "to integrate Soul more in the world through sharing my wealth" just got a boost of the most delicious blasts of Air, Earth, Fire, Water and of course Spirit, delivered with passion and the wisdom of direct experience."
~ Rev. Dr. JoyBeth Lufty, Sacred Dance Guild President and Author

"Realizing that everyone was born with the ability to bring our dreams into reality has changed the way I view the world. I now have a calm inner knowing that I can have whatever I desire. The insights and skill that I have gained with Natural Rhythms have opened doors in my life that I thought were forever closed. My life is now on a trajectory with a lot more love and peace in it."
~ Tammy Huber-Wilkins MD, Natural Rhythms Expert

"Have you ever felt like you live your life "outside of your body", disconnected from the here and now? I have and reconnecting to nature using the tools and wisdom of the elements as taught by the Natural Rhythms Institute has assisted me to feel all my aliveness and bring into fruition things I had only dreamed of before doing this work."
~ Judy Keating, MA, Natural Rhythms Expert

"Through Natural Rhythms I experienced a rite of passage where I fully integrated the elements, Earth, Air, Fire, Water and Spirit. They are living energies that nourish and sing to my soul! There was an ahh ha moment when I realized that my training as a Feng Shui Consultant had been the initiation phase of working with the elemental world. Natural Rhythms took me even deeper into feeling, hearing, seeing, smelling and touching the beauty of Mother Nature and the essence of Divine Spirit."
~ Paula York, Natural Rhythms Expert

"The elemental teachings through Natural Rhythms has given me a wonderful model to help my clients understand how to grow their wealth in alignment with natural world."
~ Mackey McNeill, CPA, Natural Rhythms Expert

"As an Ob-Gyn Physician, I use the natural rhythms of the wheel of the year and the moon almost daily in my professional life. The cycles of initiation and growth followed by rest and renewal are powerful tools for women's education and empowerment. Whether I'm framing a discussion on PMS or fertility or menopausal symptoms, I find there is wisdom to share in the Natural Rhythms and Elemental teachings."
~ Claudia Harsh, MD, Natural Rhythms Expert

"Natural Rhythms has helped me deepen my connection to my body. The value of aligning the body with the elements is hard to describe. I will say, at a time when life is moving very fast and it can be hard to keep up with the natural pace of the world, slowing down to connect with the elements helps me move into the world with ease and grace."
~ Leslie Clayton, Founder and director Body Awareness Studio, Natural Rhythms Expert

"Working with the natural elements through Natural Rhythms has enriched my personal and professional life. As a mental health professional I use the powerful the elements to assist clients in finding the source of pain they are experiencing, to solve issues they are struggling with and to experience the wonderful gifts of the natural world."
~ Helen Magers, LPCC, Natural Rhythms Expert

"The wisdom teachings of the elements have given me a deeper perspective through which to view every aspect of business and life. Through Natural Rhythms I am keenly aware of nature's timing and my own timing of expansion and contraction. With this understanding I am capable of maximizing every life experience."
~ Chantal Debrosse, Natural Rhythms Expert

Dedicated to Mother Nature.

Contents

Chapter 1

Frustrated, Dried up, Burned out, and Fiercely Craving Feminine Nourishment

Lisa Michaels

Sitting across the circle from me is yet another woman who, despite her career and life success, feels emotionally drained, burned out, out of touch, depressed, and down right empty. Frustrated because she feels dried up with all the endless doing and producing. She fiercely craves the nourishment of feminine ways of being.

No matter her sexual preference, she appreciates men, but she doesn't want to be one nor continue to replicate old strictly-male models of business and leadership. She actively wants to work in co-creative partnership with the masculine principle from a grounded juicy feminine perspective. She wants more out of life, she just doesn't want to achieve it in the old way. She wants to clear any codependent need to fit into purely masculine models, as well as strengthen her self-esteem and find her feminine voice and power.

She chooses to learn more about applying the principles of the organic natural world and creation to her leadership in order to support the environment and the generations to come. She actively seeks new models of cooperation, collaboration, growth, guidance, and focus. She wants to use her intuition, emotions, and relationship skills in business in as many ways as she uses her head to think things through. She wants to be successful and wealthy as well as live in harmony and right relationship with the natural world. She longs for her passion, purpose, and prosperity to be replenished in ways that fulfill her. And she yearns to rediscover her innate power of creation and authentic feminine leadership skills.

This deep hunger for the feminine essence in creative sacred union with masculine principle propels many women to seek the balance of their inner feminine, but it also impacts men. I've been sitting with women, like the one I've just described, in workshop after workshop for the last 12 years. While my programs have primarily filled with women, the men who have participated are also starved for the soul-filling essence of feminine creative energy and the natural world.

This innate longing calls to women and men from all sorts of careers paths, lifestyles, as well as ethnic and spiritual backgrounds. What they all have in common is that once they begin to open to the experience of learning from and connecting to Nature's Living Pulsating Field of Creation they begin to feel rejuvenated. As they start to listen to Nature's guiding wisdom, they find that their personal and professional creative capacity grows. Consistently, they find the principles of Nature can be applied to any area of life and the areas they focus on begin to improve. And these energies will do the same for you.

Based on where you place your focus and apply your energy you can:

- begin to prosper and thrive financially in more soul-filled ways.
- observe that your personal and professional relationships and communications are improving as you understand the elemental energies found in Nature.
- create more inner harmony and balance by aligning with both active and receptive energies.
- direct your intention for health and wellness in naturally supportive ways.
- find your purpose and passion expanding as you fully express your essence.
- strengthen your authentic leadership abilities as you nourish your inner feminine.
- dynamically direct the creation energies of your business and life for organic success.
- develop your inner abilities to expand your natural personal power.
- become more effective in each realm: physical, emotional, mental, action, and spiritual.

The rich content in this book will help you gain some vital support from nature for the organic growth of your creations and strengthen your inner abilities to powerfully expand your business and life success. Each chapter focuses on a specific way of utilizing the elemental forces or Nature's rhythms to enhance your ability to thrive in a certain area of life. The chapters were created by women who have worked with these energies in my workshops for years, until they became experts themselves.

They will share with you numerous ways that tapping into the dynamic creative energy of Nature can help you navigate life changes with more grace and ease, moving you from dried up to filled up.

Chapter 2

Tap Into Nature's Pulse of Creation and Rejuvenate Your Feminine Essence

Lisa Michaels

Look deep into nature, and then you will understand
everything better.
Albert Einstein

When it comes to creation, Nature constantly models the process, the cycles, and tools you need to bring anything into being if you are only paying attention. She will fill you up with her vital creative essence if you consciously open to her nourishment. When you connect to the energies they will inform you directly.

Immersing yourself even for small periods of time in the natural world is enlivening, balancing, and healing because you are involved in the pulsation of a very alive creation matrix. The more conscious you are about opening to this living energy, the more it can support you. And when you tune into it, this energy can guide you. Start noticing the difference of being inside and outside this force by feeling into the creation matrix in the natural world. Let yourself experience the tremendous aliveness found there.

Nature can and will energize your ability to think in innovative and creative ways about how to effectively transform any situation in which you may find yourself. When you need creative insights to enliven any area of your life, go spend time in the rich pulsating living field of creation found in Nature.

By deepening your capacity to listen to the wisdom and guidance found in Nature, you will discover ways to access more intuition, awareness, and insight that can direct you in every area of life. While each of the authors in this book will guide you in discovering the impact that aligning with Nature and her natural rhythms can have on your life, your primary teachers for these concepts will be your relationship to the archetypal energies of Nature itself—Earth, Water, Air, Fire, Spirit and their organic rhythmic cycles.

You receive a tremendous gift when you learn from the forces of Nature. They have so much to teach you when you open to their wisdom. Each outer force in nature corresponds to an internal energy, and they function with your consciousness and life in the same way they hold the world in form. Earth guides and informs you in the physical realm, Water in the feeling-emotional realm, Air in the mental realm, Fire in the action realm, while Spirit flows through all of them like the glue of creation.

Together the elements of Earth, Water, Air, Fire, and Spirit weave the creation fabric of the world and, if you are listening, they will teach you to apply their principles in the creation of your own life. You will see your inner nature functions just like Nature as a dynamically creative force. The more you become attuned to all the energies you work with and that work with you, the clearer you can become regarding what you bring forth in life, as well as how you respond to what comes to you. You learn to receive external events outside of your control from a space of grace, love, and compassion in addition to actively choosing to direct your life from a powerful internal position.

Each elemental force of Nature has the capacity to meet you right where you are in your development. If you are brand new to working with the elements or if you have years of experience, they will always take you to your next learning edge. Once you master a skill with an element, it will begin taking you to your next level of growth; collectively, they will help you deepen your capacity to work with all of them together in a unified field. A unified field is when all of the elements align in creation, assisting you to easily bring your desires into being. When you know how to direct each element individually and then learn to align them all together in a unified creation field, you cultivate powerful creation abilities.

These amazing energies will become your allies and will help you develop internal powers so that you can actively create anything in your life. These forces are also living energies. As such, they really appreciate connection, respect, and honoring. They especially appreciate being listened to, just like anyone else in your life—from your friends to your children and your mate. And because they are alive, you can develop a beautiful reciprocal relationship with them. The stronger your respectful connection is to them, the more they will assist you in aligning and bringing forth your creations.

When a tree branches up and out, it must create more solid roots to stabilize its expanding outer growth. In order for you to expand your abilities in the outer world, you need to deepen your root system, or your inner skills. You may have to learn new things or expand your capacity to do things in order to stabilize your growth and bring your creations into being. Sometimes developing strong roots means you have to clear things out, like having to move a rock (or old energies) out of the way to allow the roots to grow deeper.

Let me give you an example. Let's say you have a dream of become a speaker and author, and you've never done either of those things. You would need to learn quite a few new skills in order to expand into this desire. You might also need to clear old emotional patterns from childhood about how visible you can be in the world or how much success you can attain in order to develop more stable roots in this area. I've certainly had to do both of these things—learn new skills and deep clearing—with each level of business development I have taken on; so have each of these Natural Rhythms expert authors. Expanding your abilities in any area means you need to learn new skills and clear out old beliefs or feelings that have kept you feeling limited in the past, so that you can fully open and expand.

To find out more about the elements and their rhythmic cycles download a FREE Natural Rhythms Starter Kit today at <u>http://naturalrhythms.org</u> and read the *Dance of Creation* chapter.

http://naturalrhythms.org/

Trusting in Nature's Rhythmic Cycles

The elements are extremely powerful forces. While they can assist you in the creation of beauty, magnificence, success, and creative expression, it is important to remember that these same forces are also the forces of destruction. They will teach you how to apply their energies for creation and help you know what to do with them should you experience destruction.

Let's take a forest fire, for example. While a devastating force, a forest fire creates tremendous new life. In the same way, it is critical to know how to align with creation no matter what is happening in your life. Perhaps when something (loss of a job) or someone (death or divorce) leaves your life or you experience an actual elementally destructive force (earthquake, flood, fire), you want to know how to heal from that experience and to be able to redirect your energy toward creation.

In ordinary times, the natural flow of constant change in our lives is gradual and often barely noticed. With the subtle physical changes from 30 years to 40, the move from one home to another or one season to the next, you flow through the changes without giving them much attention. You can even trust in the transition to death if it comes to those elders around you, as you expect it. You experience the loss, heal, and then go on with life. You know instinctively and from experience that the nature of life around you constantly moves and expresses in rhythms and cycles.

What shakes your trust, comfort, and security is sudden change: walking into the office one day to learn you don't have a job anymore; your mate delivering divorce papers when s/he hasn't discussed it with you; an accident or event that abruptly changes your life; or finding yourself in the middle of a natural disaster. It's one thing when you want a change—to release what you are ready to let go of—but to be suddenly thrust by an external force into a vast expanse of change can bring all of your human vulnerabilities to the surface.

It's in those moments when you need to draw on all the inner resources you can. Your ability to create success in life isn't just about actively directing the forces of creation from a powerful internal position, although that is essential. You also need the ability to manage and respond to cycles of change in the world around you from as much grace, love, and compassion as possible.

Interestingly enough, the elemental forces can help you do just that. Each element (Earth, Water, Air, Fire, and Spirit) develops your core strength in powerful ways that assist you in directing the energy of creation in your life as well as supporting your ability to manage external events. Learning how each one functions and learning to work with their tools can help you navigate when you find yourself in a sea of change.

Staying connected to Earth's changing rhythmic motion and fundamental principles will help you live in greater harmony with the world around you and, in turn, develop increased inner wisdom, balance, and peace. The pace of modern technology-filled life sometimes makes it challenging to find what you need most to balance yourself. Everywhere you go, from the gym to the local restaurant, media broadcasts bombard you. Computers bring an overload of information from the Internet and e-mail 24/7, and people can call your cell phones or text you anywhere at anytime. While technology helps you in so many ways, it can also disconnect you from the place where you can most easily balance—the natural world.

Nature's calming and healing energy helps you align with your own inner nature, which balances you vibrationally, thus maximizing your capacity to handle the stresses of this increasingly technology-filled world. Not only does Nature harmonize your energy field, her fundamental principles increase your wisdom and teach you about your life. As Earth's seasons turn and change, you learn from Nature that your life, too, follows this same rhythm of constant transformation. Sometimes the shifts in life express in a subtle and gradual change and sometimes they are quick and impactful. Yet the undercurrent of motion keeps the energy turning.

Earth's constant rotation through the seasons of the year provides a wonderful organic teaching of the natural balance process through Nature's examples of light and dark, life and death. Starting with the dark, fallow time in winter, the earth rests and rejuvenates. It turns to the gradual warming of the soil with the light of the sun until it heats enough for planting in the spring and then moves into the full brightness of the summer growing time. Then, the light gradually recedes to the fall harvest, finally diminishing as the crops die and the earth settles into its period of dark winter rejuvenation once again.

For most people, life follows this same pattern: we gestate in the womb's darkness, are born, grow from childhood into adulthood and then into elder years, and move on to our death and the next expression. The growth and change, as well as the light and dark phases of your life, happen over time as you move from phase to phase.

If you learn from nature you realize that too much light and outer world activity leaves little time for rest or quiet and burns out your systems. Busy external lives require balance found during the darkness, the peaceful rest times. Quiet inner time creates the place where you are receptive to inner voice of Spirit, and where seeds of your desires are planted, developed, and grown. You create inner balance when you learn to work with and appreciate the light and bright times of life that bring you into the outer world for growth, joy, and creativity, as well as those times that take you deep into your inner darkness for rejuvenation and physical and emotional healing.

Finding a wavelike rhythm and routine reaps great rewards
and can actually be a surprisingly powerful act of
Extreme Self-Care.
Cheryl Richardson

Discovering ways to honor both the light and dark times of life creates more trust in life itself. Nature exists in a constant state of balancing light and dark as well as creating the new and letting go of the old. When you spend enough time connected to the natural world and the rhythm of nature, you are filled with this understanding and the grounded wisdom of Earth. Nature softly reminds you that life and death are interconnected just as are the light and the dark. Each year spring follows winter. Nature's processes take time, and you cannot rush her season. However, when you listen to her, you hear her urge you to trust that following the time to rest and heal once again comes a time to celebrate once again.

Nature is the most powerful model for organic growth and living sustainable systems. Even when she shifts into winter's rest, she's always got that living pulse happening. So when you align your life, health, wealth, passion, career, leadership, and personal power with her creation pulse you can actively organically flourish while also deeply nourishing your essence.

Connecting and Centering with the Elements

Even when reading about the elemental forces of Nature, it helps to consciously take a moment to center and connect with them. So take a deep breath and move your spine and your shoulders around. Then really move your body as much as you can. Then invite the divine source that flows through life and Nature's elements—some people call it Great Spirit, God, Goddess, or other names—into you. Simply call on and connect with the spiritual realm.

Now honor and connect to Earth and your physical body, and send appreciation to your legs, arms, and hands. Next imagine putting your hands on the ground outside and giving thanks and connecting to the Earth Mother.

Connect to Water and the beautiful emotional realm inside yourself. Appreciate how fabulous it is that water nourishes the planet and your creations. Feel into Water, honor it, and invite it to work with you.

Now take a breath and give thanks to for the precious breath of life. Connect to Air and the mental realm, your ability to think and vision.

Now feel into Fire, the sun, the solar force, your own energy and life force. Invite Fire to work with you today.

Creating an honoring connection to these sacred forces assists you as you open to learn from them. Enjoy.

Chapter 3

Build Enduring Wealth by Claiming the Feminine Power of Money

Mackey McNeill

Metamorphosis in the Garden

No journey carries one far unless it goes an equal distance into the world within.
Lillian Smith

We all operate on a continuum when it comes to money. Some love to manage it, some prefer to ignore it. We love to save, we love to spend. One money style isn't necessarily better than the other, and most of us fall somewhere between the two extremes. The key is to embrace a style that enables our relationship with money to work well for our individual needs, otherwise known as our *emotional/money DNA*. Like personality, emotional/money DNA is formed early in life. Once established, it becomes how we *see*, *feel*, and *behave* around money. The best position to be in with money is one of balance: some spending, some saving, some management, some avoidance, some indifference, and some rules. This chapter is about finding the joy in achieving that balance.

I didn't know all this when I started investing at the age of 18. My primary belief was that money equaled safety, so I needed to have lots of it, save it, and be really good at it. After college, I built a successful business as a CPA. When I decided to add personal financial planning to my services, I became a Registered Investment Advisor and a Personal Financial Specialist. At this point, I began to see that knowing how money worked was a necessary, but insufficient skill, if I was going to truly help people. I'd gained more credentials, but what my staff and I needed was to better understand people.

My next step was to learn how people's personalities impact their relationship with wealth and money. Our personalities develop early in life and remain fairly consistent. The same, it turns out, is true for our money personalities (aka *emotional/money DNA*). As my staff and I started actively using this new knowledge with our clients, layers of understanding about how they were relating to their money and wealth became clearer. We were becoming more effective and our collaborations more impactful.

One of our key discoveries was that each client's internal money beliefs were reflected in their external money behavior with unerring accuracy. As within, so without. This meant that learning self-reflection *had* to be an essential part of the process through which we guided them. What I didn't foresee is that because we teach what we need to learn, I was going to have to look in the mirror, too. And as I looked within I discovered how my natural propensity to take care of others was getting in my own way with money. I worked very hard to find my point of balance and joy between saving and spending so I could experience pleasure from my wealth, rather than stress.

This inner work made it clear that I needed to fine-tune how we were working with our clients. I could see their financial situations clearly and direct them to do this or that differently, but *they* weren't being brought into the process enough. The resulting financial plan couldn't be organically *theirs* because it was coming from *outside* of them. If they wanted to change their relationship to money, they would have to change too. Soon we were no longer simply crafting solutions *for* them, but instead leading them along the path to discovering their own solutions. While this shift was invaluable in helping our clients, I was unknowingly poised to receive a huge infusion of insight about people and money from a rather unlikely source.

Earth, Water, Air, Fire and . . . money?! Surprisingly, the next step in my personal journey in learning about money was presented by Mother Nature herself. She taught me that the natural world—the elements of *Earth*, *Water*, *Air*, and *Fire* with the linchpin of *Spirit*—provides an organic system for understanding every aspect of our lives, including money. This life-changing lesson came to me from Lisa Michaels and the series of coursework I completed through her *Natural Rhythms* Institute.

With this munificent gift of understanding from the natural world, I began to compare growing wealth to growing a garden. If you can understand this earth-based process (gardening), you can also understand the process of growing money. You are part of the natural world, as is your money. All wealth comes from Earth's physical plane. The way money works in your life isn't esoteric, it's concrete. This turned out to be a powerful, clear analogy that took the mystery out of money for our clients. They truly understood and embraced it.

This is how I now live my life—in context, delightfully integrated with Nature and Spirit, aligned with well-being and wholeness. As a result, my work with my clients is more effective, fun, enjoyable, and enlivening. My clients have more ease and grace around money. Connecting with the natural world brings us more joy, more fulfillment . . . simply *more*.

Many elements contributed to the creation of the self-discovery process, *The Prosperity Experience,* including my acumen in the world of finance, immersion into money behavior, and the transformational experience of working with the elements and Spirit. Elegant in its simplicity, once it was implemented it tripled our business through word of mouth.

Summary
Our relationship to money is a living relationship, and all of the elements must be active and integrated. We can't just *think* our way to wealth. We must align our emotions, intentions, and actions. We can work harder and longer around the money in our lives or we can have ease through integration. It's all about choices . . . and gardens.

Planting a Wealth Garden

> Gardens are a form of autobiography.
> Sydney Eddison

At the core of creation there is yin and yang, heaven and earth, inhaling and exhaling. Wealth, as a part of creation, works the same way in its expansion and contraction, spending and saving, ebb and flow. As within, so without. You have to find that balance within yourself for your money to be effective.

I'm going to give you a set of steps that will help you understand how to build a balanced wealth garden and how to find joy in what you grow. They are:

- *Setting* the intention for your garden (using *Air*).
- *Testing* the fertility of your garden (using *Water*).
- *Identifying* specific goals for your garden (using *Earth*).
- *Establishing* a plan to reach your goals (using *Earth*).
- *Executing* your plan (using *Fire*).
- *Aligning* with the heart of your garden (using *Spirit*).

Setting the Intention (Air)

What kind of a garden do you want to grow? What is your wealth intention? The element of *Air*, the realm of thought, comes to assist you in conceiving and writing down your intention for your wealth garden. We all have intentions around our money whether it's conscious or unconscious, written or in our mind. You can think of your wealth intention as an expression of your overall purpose for money in your life and the values you hold around your money.

For example, what do you suppose the wealth intention is for Bill Gates and Warren Buffet? They have both pledged to give away the majority of their earnings to charitable organizations. Their wealth intention is, "To change the world through philanthropy." My own wealth garden intention right now is, "To create and enjoy my wealth."

All of your subsequent decisions about money must align with your overarching intention so that your garden can flourish. It's also important to check in periodically with your intention to see if it has shifted, in which case it's a good idea to take the time to re-write it. It will undoubtedly shift throughout your lifetime as your financial situation changes and evolves.

These wealth intentions are like a template or an overlay that you use to verify whether or not your money choices are aligned with your financial well-being.

Here are a few more examples of intention statements:

- I live a comfortable, financially independent life style that allows me to be effortlessly generous to my Source, myself, and others with ease, grace and joy.
- My intention is to fully embody the role of family matriarch, to lead through love, strength, and wisdom.
- I choose to experience financial freedom through living simply and graciously within my means.
- I intend to be a positive role model for the young people in our extended family. I intend to be healthy, active, engaged, and remembered with affection.

Your wealth garden intention is so important because without it you tend to make decisions that are off-focus. They're not bad decisions; they're just not the best decisions for your situation. With a clear, current intention you can hold it up to your decisions and see if they are a good match. Here's an example:

I have clients who tell me their intention is to live simply. Then they tell me they want a lake house. This could still be within their intention or it could just add more stress. It's okay either way, but they need to be clear. Having an established intention allows them to examine any conflicts they might set up in their lives around money. Again, it's not a right or wrong, but when the time comes to take action, they don't want to be working against themselves.

Essence

In setting your wealth intention, you're making a commitment to yourself. Take some time to be sure of your intention. You might want to sleep on it or think about setting it aside for a few days. You're making a commitment to keep your word to yourself in order to align all the subsequent steps of building your wealth garden with this intention. You're also sending out *Air* waves from this intention, making it known to Spirit, God, the

Universe, heaven (*whatever terms works for you*) how you want to relate to your money. Get clear.

Testing the Fertility (Water)

You've set your intention. The next step is testing the composition of your soil. If you're going to build a garden, you have to take a soil sample first to find out what's true about the soil, to test for its *fertility*—is it low in nitrogen? Does it have enough phosphorus, too much clay or iron? If so, that doesn't mean that it's bad soil. It just means that some things are going to grow well in it while some things are not. If the soil's fertility is not right for what you choose to move forward anyway, you will grow disappointments.

Your emotional/money DNA—what you made true about money when you were a child—is the fertility content in your wealth garden. By cultivating self-awareness of your emotional/money DNA (*testing the fertility*) and knowing what's in your emotional body around money, you will gain the ability to make choices.

To test the fertility in your wealth garden you're going to call on *Water*, the element of emotions. Our emotions come from what scientists call the "old" part of our brain, the part that has no access to language and makes decisions based on the watery realm of emotions. The "new" part of our brain is analytical. We use language from this analytical part of our brain to justify our choices made by the emotional part of our brain. We think our decisions are coming from a rational place, but they originate in our emotional brain. Accurate soil fertility testing in your wealth garden depends on an accurate assessment of your emotional/money DNA.

Parts of your wealth garden fertility, your emotional/money DNA, have been passed down to you from your parents, grandparents, and other significant adult figures. Whatever shows up in your soil fertility test is partially influenced by you, but a lot of it came from somebody else. So you have to ask, "Do I want to keep this soil and grow my wealth in it, or are there some things I want to take out of the soil or amend the soil fertility composition in some way?"

You want your soil to be the most fertile for your particular wealth intention. For example:

- If you know that you have primarily a spend-money DNA, you don't have to give it up altogether, it just means that you have to be aware of it in yourself and moderate it so you can also enjoy the saving aspect of your wealth.
- If saving is the only thing you know that's safe, then everything else is going to be fearful. If you're going to have joy around money, you have to shift that fear, and you can't shift it if you're not aware of it.

There are many different tools to help you identify and shift your emotional/money DNA including working with the staff at my company, *Mackey Advisors*™, or reading my book, *The Intersection of Joy and Money*.

Essence
If the only thing that can grow in your soil is rhododendrons and that's what you *want* to have in your garden that's fine. If you want to grow something else in your garden, then you need to work with your soil. Likewise, in your wealth garden, the soil fertility has to be the right match for what you want to produce. If the soil's not quite right, get your hoe and turn it over, till in whatever needs to change with the power of self-awareness, and you'll be ready to produce the wealth garden you've envisioned in your intention.

Identifying Goals (Earth)

When establishing a garden you need to know your desired outcome. Are you going to eat from this garden? Is it going to be a flower cutting garden? If you're going to plant a spring garden so you can have salads, then you need to be thinking about getting busy and planning in the springtime because you're not going to be growing lettuce in the summer when it's not likely to be successful.

In your wealth garden, you must set your intentions and have an understanding of your emotional/money DNA before you will be ready to identify specific goals. You will call on the concrete support of *Earth* to help you define your goals. Different from intentions, goals are measurable and they have a time frame. For example:

- I want to retire or be financially independent by age 65 (*measurable*). At a specific age this is what's going to happen in my life and I can determine if I'm going to get there or not.
- I want to send my child to Harvard in the year 20__ (*measurable*). I can figure out how to accomplish this goal by taking into account how many years I have to save, as well as a projected cost of tuition.

Define the measurable outcomes you want from your wealth garden. What are the markers of success you will measure by? Whatever your goals are—for retirement, for your children's education, for buying a vacation home, for a special trip—set them down in writing, define the outcomes, measurements, and time frames. This is a time to clearly state financial goals in all areas of your life—career, investments, retirement, vacations, education, home, special purchases.

Essence
Goals can make us uneasy. An intention can have just enough of an ethereal element to not threaten our equilibrium. Goals take us right up next to that wily border between thought and physical action. We know we're going to be called upon to do something. Remember, when you learned to walk you took baby steps. It's the same thing in learning about money—you have to take baby steps and do what works for you. Embrace your goals. Get them on paper.

Establishing a Plan (Earth)

You have your goals. The next step is for you to develop a plan to meet your goals. *Earth* provides you with a tangible structure in the form of step-by-step plans for each goal. This system of planned steps supports you in taking specific actions in a specific sequence. How many steps you'll have to take to get to one goal is not necessarily the same as the distance to another goal. It's based on the complexity of the goal and the length of time that you're going to be interacting with that goal.

Your short-term goals have short-term plans and your long-term goals have long-term plans. For example:

- If you're planning a garden for summer, it's going to be a short-term plan, a single season. If you're saving for a new refrigerator, that's like a summer garden—you're going to enjoy it and eat it!
- If you're planning a forest garden, that could be 30 years in the making. Planting a retirement garden is a lot like planting a forest garden—it takes a long time to grow and you're going to be using it for a long time.

Human beings sometimes have such a hard time with long-term goals because we're more focused on today, tomorrow, and the day after that—short-term objectives. Long-term goals can seem so far out there and not have much to do with you in current terms, so the temptation is to postpone taking action. As a result, you're faced with trying to achieve a long-term goal in a short amount of time. For example:

- You're fifty years old. You begin thinking about saving money for retirement. It's not impossible at this point, but you haven't been planting any trees and you want a forest garden. You're going to start planting trees now, but what do you think is going to happen? You're going to have a small, immature garden.
- If you started 25 years ago, perhaps you couldn't have planted a whole hill of trees, but you could have planted one or two trees each year. After 30 years you might not have a complete forest, but you'd be in a much better position that someone who had postponed doing any planting at all.

If you're trying to figure out how to pay your light bill or if you are a young adult, it's hard to understand how or why you should be moving toward long-term financial goals. The way you get there is by taking it one step at a time. The *Earth* realm is the place for systems, structures, and forms, so when you have a plan in place—*I'm going to save this amount from every pay check*—then the plan itself informs what your next action is. You follow the plan. Without having the plan and the steps, you're likely to keep going on default and end up not meet your goals.

The question I'm asked most often concerning goals is, "How much money should I/we be saving?"

- If you're not saving any, start with five or ten dollars a pay check. Don't jump right to the most you think you *could* save.
- If you've been saving a regular amount successfully for some time, consider a small increase. Keep it at a level at which you can continue to be successful.

By saving a small amount regularly, you're learning *how* to save, experiencing doing it well, and gaining necessary encouragement. *Earth* helps you learn this kind of consistency. Things take time with Earth, just as in gardening, and you'll get better as you go along. Using *Water* you are examining and shifting your emotional/money DNA to create success, and that in turn breeds more success.

One of the things we're emphatic about with our clients is weaning them away from comparisons. People judge themselves and others around money and our ego-brains are addicted to comparing. For example, you may avoid taking stock of your financial situation because you're starting off from a perspective of feeling defeated. Maybe you read in some magazine that you should be saving 25% of your take-home pay and you know that's not going to happen. Perhaps you read in a magazine about a couple who are saving large amounts of money using the latest XYZ saving method, and it doesn't feel like a match for you. Regardless of the reason for your initial feeling of defeat, resisting the urge to compare yourself to others can make the process much more productive. Just do the $10 today. Don't try to match what somebody else is doing. This is personal. And with your plan in place, you've got your own logic, sequencing, and patterns that work for YOU.

Essence

Without a plan, you'll just wander around your wealth garden and won't accomplish your goals. When you know what the steps are, you can focus. You don't have to overwhelm yourself with looking at the big goals, just follow your step-by-step plan. This can be very freeing and help reduce financial worry. Check off the steps on your to-do list as you go along, and remember to be your *own* measuring stick. Let go of comparing and praise yourself for your successes!

Executing your Plan (Fire)

You've set your intention, self-assessed your emotional/money DNA, established your goals, and have a plan for reaching them. Now it's time to get in motion, and *Fire*, the element of action, will help you do that. Your relationship with money is a relationship that's alive, so it requires your attention, which is a form of energy that helps your garden grow.

For example, say you've committed to saving that $10 per pay check. Let's start there.

- Open a savings account.
- Make your first deposit.
- Celebrate!

You've started taking the actual steps you assigned for that goal. It's like planning your garden and you have everything ready. Now you have to go out and put the seeds in the ground at the right time, or you won't have a garden!

You don't just put the seeds in and go away. You need to water, weed, and tend your garden. You have to go outside and see what's happening. If pests are invading, you have to take corrective action. Likewise, you don't just put your money in an account or investment tool and think you don't have to worry about it anymore. You have to continue to interact with your money for it to work in your life the way you want it to. You have to go back and look at your steps, your plans, your goals, and your intention. Don't obsess, but do check in periodically.

Essence

As you move into action, pay close attention to what may get in your way. If your plan is too challenging for you, you might self-sabotage as you begin to execute it. The feelings that may come up as you move into action are important clues. Perhaps you've stretched yourself too far with a particular goal. You may need to spend some time looking at the feelings and see how they relate to your emotional/money DNA. See what beliefs are still in play that you thought you shifted (*moved out of your soil*) and what you need to do to moderate them a little more.

You want to have all the elements of your wealth garden working together at this point so you can say, "Wow, it's really happening and I'm getting there!"

Aligning with your Heart (Spirit)

When you make a purchase, you're expressing your values. Sometimes you think about it, and sometimes you don't. Sometimes it matters more than other times. In your wealth garden, you can sow many kinds of seeds. When you select seeds that are aligned with your values, you feel a connection to Spirit that is solid and affirming. Again, this is not an area for comparisons. One person's junk is another person's treasure. Here's an example from my own life:

When I started writing my book, *The Intersection of Joy and Money*, one of the things I explored further was the concept of socially responsible investing. The individuals and companies who follow this school of thought have a triple bottom line: people, planet, and profit. In other words, their money is focused in ways that align with their greater intention. Another way individuals can align their money with their wealth intention in a socially responsible way is making fair trade purchases. This means producers in developing countries receive equitable payment for their goods while conforming to higher social and environmental standards for their communities.

When I looked at my intention for my wealth garden (to create and enjoy my wealth), I realized I wanted to shift some of my investments so that I was supporting companies that are green or have more of a clear intention of being a green company, and producing a lower carbon footprint on the Earth. Now, this doesn't have anything to do with building my wealth, but it makes me feel better about my investments. Knowing that I'm doing good while I'm building my wealth allows me to feel aligned with Spirit. Making my personal decisions with an awareness of how they might impact the other beings of the Earth is in alignment with my wealth intention.

Bonus: As your awareness of how and where you spend your dollars continues to grow, more opportunities to express this part of your wealth intention will show up.

Essence
Take baby steps. Do one thing differently today that will bring Spirit and your wealth intention into alignment. Do what feels good to YOU, not what you've been told to do, or what someone else is doing. Let your emotions (*Water*) tell you how your choices and actions are reflecting the way you live and interact with money. One of the reasons people have so much trouble with money is that they haven't been taught to integrate it with the whole of their lives and who they are. Monitor (*Earth, Water, Air, Fire*) your wealth garden. Compare your results to your plans and see what adjustments may be needed.

Decision Making in the Wealth Garden

Once you make a decision, the universe conspires
to make it happen.
Ralph Waldo Emerson

Our method of making decisions—remember this is part of our personality DNA and our emotional/money DNA—is primarily *reactive*, coming from the "old" emotional part of our brain. *Integrated* decision-making inserts a pause into our emotional reactivity so we can think through our decisions and avoid costly mistakes. The integrated decision-making process says, "When I'm making BIG decisions, I'm going to look at my plan and see how this decision is going to impact all parts of my life." For example, an economic downturn is a time of fear. Some people sell everything they have and turn it into cash. That's *reactive* decision making. The fact is, if they stay in the stock market, they'll be better off. What ultimately happens is a loss of money as a result of reactive decision-making.

If you think of your investments as a part of your bigger wealth plan, then you're aware when you invest that there are going to be ups and downs. That's how investments work. They are cyclical—the stock market, the real estate market, the products/services market, and so on. If you deepen your understanding of this as you define your goals and increase your money understanding, then you know this kind of volatility is part of investing. Then when the time comes, rather than simply reacting, you're going to stick with your plan. This is where you can really experience the importance of having a system in place because it holds you (*Earth*) and keeps you from making reactive decisions. Instead, you're empowered to make integrated decisions: "Okay, I know this is how investing works. It's a seasonal cycle and right now it's winter."

Our planet has seasons: winter, spring, summer, and fall. Sometimes if we don't have a cold enough winter, we don't have as nice a summer. The cycle is always turning from one season to the next. Granted, we can know the timing of these earthly seasons a little more clearly than we can for the economic seasons, but they are there nonetheless. The stock market's winter season is called a recession. We have expansion *and* we have recession.

I tell my clients that to think that a recession is abnormal is ridiculous. It just IS. To react against it is like reacting against winter. It's not going to make winter leave any faster or summer come any sooner. When it's wintertime for our various investments, we have to do those things that we do in winter—wear extra clothes, snuggle down, keep some cash handy, make other choices, and wait for spring. In economic cycles, the thing we don't know is *when*. To help yourself sit with uncertainty, go back to your investment plan, recognize that this is normal, and wait. When you contemplate the *recession-expansion* analogy and relate your various investments to the seasons, can you feel a change in how you feel emotionally and physically?

Integrated decision making gives you a way to set a course, keep in balance, and continue moving forward toward your goals, and it's all about Y-O-U. You're focused on yourself, YOUR plan, and what YOU want. Focus on creating that and avoiding the comparison game which can cause you to revert into reactive mode. It's not about what anyone else is doing. Owning your wealth garden and standing in the strength of your wealth intention is a very different position than the one from which most of us make our decisions around money.

Essence

To find the joy in your wealth garden, stay out of the chaos in the world around you. Turn off the TV and don't listen to all the screaming heads. Focus on YOUR intention, goal, plan, and actions. Focus within.

Common Wealth Gardening Mistakes

> *There are no mistakes, no coincidences, all events are*
> *blessings given to us to learn from.*
> *Elizabeth Kubler-Ross*

It's good to know what doesn't work so you can choose what does. Here are three pivotal mistakes many people make in relation to their wealth garden.

1. *Not having and using an integrated decision-making model.* When you do have and use an integrated decision-making model, it means that you:
   - have a clear intention,
   - understand your emotional/money DNA,
   - have clear goals and a step-by-step plan to meet them, are executing your goals in alignment with the elements to create what you want.

   In addition, it means that you see the different aspects of your wealth garden—insurance, investments, cash flow, debt, and so on—as parts of the whole. You are not thinking of these as separate, so you will be making integrated decisions *within* the whole.

2. *Not having and using a disciplined, integrated investment plan.* Asset allocation is an example of this type of investment plan and the approach that I teach. You can use this model yourself or hire an advisor that uses the model. Very simply, an asset allocation model is deciding *before* you start your investing what percentages of your assets are going to be in different asset classes. For example, you might have 50% of your assets in stocks and 50% in bonds. This means no matter what happens you're always going to keep that ratio. If you get 60% in stocks, you're going to sell some of your stocks and buy bonds.

This is a model that respects the elements, respects the reality of the world, and it gives you a model to execute and within which to make your decisions. If you study investment approaches, you'll see that asset allocation as an investment discipline has lowered risks and raised returns.

What doesn't work in investing is an undisciplined, unplanned approach because it leads to making reactive decisions. What you tend to get from this approach is not necessarily what will work best for you. Here is a prime example of a client who had been using an unplanned approach, came to me for advice, and discovered (just in time) the benefits of a disciplined, integrated investment plan:

> *This gentleman came into my office and said he wanted to retire. That was his #1 goal and he wanted to retire immediately. He had about 80% of his investments in a China fund and had done phenomenally well, something like 30% returns the previous year. I said, "You know, you are ready to retire now, and the volatility of this fund is off the charts. It could go down 50% tomorrow and then how are you going to retire?" We put together a new investment plan. His plan might have been good for a 20 year old with a long time to recover, but it made no sense for a 50 year old who wanted to start living off his assets right away. Fortunately for him, we made those decisions before the 2008-09 crash which meant he actually was able to retire and stay retired. If he hadn't followed a disciplined investment plan that fit with his goals, he would probably still be working or going back to work.*

3. *Not having and using the power of the right kind of financial advisor.* Some of us are going to take care of our wealth garden completely on our own. We're going to do our own research, plan, plant, tend; everything on our own because we like it, live it, breathe it, and enjoy it. We love playing around with money. Some of us aren't like this and what happens for people in this category is that they either act like ostriches and don't make decisions, or make crazy decisions whenever they happen to stick their head up for air.

You have to look carefully and ask yourself if you're the kind of person who wants to be your own wealth advisor. If not, then you need to hire one and you need to understand *how* your advisor works. At a minimum, you need to know:

- Their philosophy and whether it aligns with yours.
- How they get paid. Ask them to explain the process so you can clearly understand it.

Many people tend to ask their friends who they use. Then they are too embarrassed to ask the necessary questions because of the association with their friend. They end up using someone who doesn't fit with their money intention.

"You know, I just hated this advisor, but my best friend loved her."
"My advisor said I always have to do it like this."

If you want an advisor who's a dictator, that wouldn't be me. I'm the person who asks what YOU want and then, together, we figure out how to get it. On the other hand, if you're not sure what you want and you want somebody that just says, do XYZ, then you *need* that kind of advisor. Again, you need to find what fits for you, your intention for your wealth garden, and your money goals.

Essence
The lack of:

- an integrated decision-making model
- a disciplined, integrated investment plan
- the power of the right kind of financial advisor

These three wealth gardening mistakes are all part of the *Earth* realm of structures, systems, and plans. If you're going to plant a garden, you have to understand your resources. You wouldn't go out to your garden with a fork in your hand. You'd walk out with a hoe or a shovel.

When you plan and plant your wealth garden, one of the things you cannot be timid about is being clear about the resources you are bringing to the table. You wouldn't plant a seed in the garden without knowing what kind of a seed it was, but you'll hire a financial advisor without really knowing what they do or how they do it. Do your homework. Be your own best advocate when it comes time to commit to a decision-making model, an investment approach, and an advisor for your wealth garden. Use your wealth intention as your template and find the matches that are best for you.

Activities to Enhance your Wealth Garden

Money is the visible sign of a universal force,
and this force in its manifestation on earth works on
the vital and physical planes and is indispensable
to the fullness of the outer life. In its origin and its true
action it belongs to the Divine.
Sri Aurobindo

This section contains some activities to help you begin thinking about your wealth garden and what you want to grow in it.

What Is My Intention For My Wealth Garden? (Air)
Experiment with writing your personal wealth intention. Use the examples in this chapter to help you get started. Write several and let them vary so you can gauge your response to them. This will help you focus in on the one that rings true.

What Is In The Fertility Of My Wealth Garden? (Water)
To help you begin to explore your emotional/money DNA, write your answer to these three questions about your relationship to money. See what comes up and journal about it.

- How do I feel about money and wealth?
- What role does money play in my life today?
- What is one thing that my experience with money has taught me?
- What is one thing I know for sure about money?

What Are My Goals For My Wealth Garden? (Earth)
What goals spring immediately to mind? Select one or two that are priorities for you and see if you can write them so that they include the necessary measurable events (amounts of money, dates, number of years, etc.)

What Plans Can I Identify To Support My Goals? (Earth)
Select one of your goals from the step above. Write down all the steps you can think of that you might need to take to reach it. Prioritize the steps into a sequential plan.

What Step Can I Take Toward One Of My Goals? (Fire)
Select one or more steps from the plan you developed in the step above. Make a commitment to complete those steps by a specific date.

How Will I Align My Heart With My Wealth Garden? (Spirit)
What values guide the way you live your life? What causes resonate with you? Do you have a personal mission? How do all of these things show up in your wealth intention or financial goals? Do one thing differently today that will bring Spirit and your wealth intention into greater alignment.

Seeking A Financial Advisor
At some point in your process, you may choose to seek a financial advisor to assist you in preparing a financial plan and making investments that support your life goals. When you hire someone to help you with your financial life, remember to delegate, not abdicate. There are a few essentials to keep in mind when working with an advisor. One is that you need to understand your advisor's advice. If you don't, ask questions. The better educated you are as a consumer the better client you will be.

Refer to Chapter 10 in The Intersection of Joy and Money for tips on finding and hiring advisors.

Summary
Before undertaking any of the activities contained in this last section, make some notes about the thoughts and feelings that came up for you as you read this chapter. Remember, feelings are important clues to the fertility of the soil that you have right now in your wealth garden. Use your notes to guide you and as you complete a suggested activity, see what surfaces and what that tells you about your emotional/money DNA. This will guide you as you begin to make shifts and get ready to plan and prosper from your wealth garden.

About Mackey McNeill

For over 30 years, Mackey's passion has been empowering individuals and business owners to take confident action in the arena of building wealth and prosperity. She is President/CEO of Mackey Advisors®, Wealth Advocates, where client's dreams become reality using their proprietary, award-winning process, The Prosperity Experience®. Mackey has the credentials to support her passion as a Certified Public Accountant, Personal Financial Specialist, Investment Advisor Representative, Certified Enneagram Teacher, and *Natural Rhythms* expert. She is the author of *The Intersection of Joy & Money,* named "Most Life Changing Book" in 2003 by the Independent Publishers Association.

About Mackey Advisors

We are Wealth Advocates! We empower confident action in our client's lives using our award-winning process, The Prosperity Experience. If you are looking for a typical transactional Investment Advisor then we probably aren't for you. Yes, we do all of that technical stuff that advisors do to make people money, but unlike most advisors we focus on you and your life goals first & foremost!

The Prosperity Experience is an interactive, hands-on process for individuals and families. It engages your emotions, commands the power of intention, establishes clear structure, and provides an action plan. Courage and a willingness to consciously create wealth and prosperity in your life are required.

When we ask our clients what The Prosperity Experience has done for them, typical responses are: freedom from worry, confidence, and reduction of conflict over money in their household, clarity, and peace of mind.

If you are looking for a wealth advocate, then we are for you! Visit www. MackeyAdvisors.com to learn more about who we are and what we do, or give us a call at (859) 331-7755.

Chapter 4

Tending Your Feminine Temple:
Use the Power of the Elements to Create Health

Claudia E. Harsh, MD

Cycles Emerge

I love cycles. I love the power of the cycle of life and birth, the awareness of the generations behind and ahead of us—stretching beyond the limits of imagination and time. I love considering a moment of time in the midst of a lifetime and consider its own cycles of birth, adolescence, growth and death. And, true confessions, I even love the month-to-month cycle of menstruation. I love the intricate hormonal dance and the microscopic handshakes and greetings that occur on a cellular level.

My awareness and love of cycles crystallized for me when I saw a woman give birth for the first time in 1981. Picture me, a first year medical student on her first clinical rotation. Most of my classmates were assigned to Family Medicine doctors or Internal Medicine doctors near the medical school—not me! My assignment took me 20 miles north of town to an Obstetrician Gynecologist (Ob/Gyn) physician's office. We saw pregnant women, menopausal women, and teenagers with a whole range of health issues. When my mentoring doctor was called to the hospital for a delivery one day, I followed along.

Hospitals weren't new to me. My father worked as a Pathologist and I frequently rode along with him on weekends or holidays. I knew laboratories—his home turf—and watched him perform autopsies and prepare surgical tissue for microscopic review. I loved his perspective that every laboratory test or piece of tissue he processed was part of a person's story and that his job was to help figure out the plotline and the characters in the story. He had a passion for order and accuracy, explaining once that his interpretations and decisions were critical to patient care.

But labor and delivery was a whole new area for me! Fetal monitors, labor graphs, women in pain, and nervous husbands . . . my senses took it all in. I stood by watching as my doctor's laboring mother pushed out her son. My mentor allowed me to put on a gown and gloves and help "catch" the baby. (He was there doing the work . . . . I just stood by in awe!) The baby cried right away and snuggled in to his mother's arms. He was the sum total of nine months of a specific egg fertilized by a specific sperm that grew in his mother's womb until the signal came to start his life in our world. The quiet nursing sounds he made and her smile captured the moment. She graciously shared her feelings about this pregnancy and how different it was from her daughter's. We explored her feelings about parenting two children now, what was going to be different, what would be the same. She talked about her job and the preparations she had made to be out for a few months. My mentor physician excused me from office hours for the rest of the day because he wisely saw she was teaching me as much (if not more) than I would learn back in his office that afternoon.

So "fast forward" through medical school and you won't be surprised to learn that I was drawn to train professionally in Ob/Gyn. Like all medical students, I rotated through Pediatrics, Surgery, Family Medicine, Ob/Gyn and Internal Medicine. I loved all of the clinical rotations, to be honest, but the practice of Ob/Gyn drew me in. After training I started a multi-specialty women's center with a colleague and in the course of my professional life delivered over a thousand babies and grew a busy and successful practice. As I mentioned in my first book, *Finding Grace and Balance in the Cycle of Life: Exploring Integrative Gynecology*[1], I felt pushed by the Western medicine model, and I couldn't explore time-consuming topics such as marital stress, pregnancy loss, or parenting a child with special needs as they come up in standard office visits. In addition, it was difficult to have a thorough discussion of nutrition and lifestyle coaching— an area that was poorly covered in my training. Through the course of my private practice I felt gradually less fulfilled and less connected to women's health and well-being. I started to see a correlation between my clients' social history and their gynecologic symptoms. More than once I noticed that the patient who needed a hysterectomy (removal of her uterus) was either in the middle of a divorce or in some sort of family crisis. I started to explore outside of my education and training for resources and tools for optimal healing.

And like many of my clients and colleagues, I felt pulled apart by responsibilities and expectations. I was balancing a busy practice and night call with my marriage and family. I began to recognize that there is a rhythm and a pattern and an underlying force of balance in our bodies. Through personal growth programs such as *Life Success Seminars*[2] I explored concepts like trust, responsibility, and forgiveness. I recognized the gifts I had been given and I started to give back to the community through established groups like the March of Dimes or by organizing and managing groups that looked to the needs of victims of domestic violence or groups that taught stress management techniques to incarcerated prostitutes looking to "start over" in their lives.

I attribute my decision to study acupuncture to a seminal dream followed by a series of coincidences. I vividly recall a meditation retreat through *Life Success Seminars* that underlined the importance of quieting my mind so that I could "hear" direction and gain focus. One particularly vivid dream came through during a meditation exercise in which I was aware of flying through space. As my attention shifted, I became aware I was riding on the back of a colorfully embroidered dragon. After the retreat was over, dragons showed up in my life in the form of birthday cards, kites and a flyer in the mail advertising the UCLA acupuncture course for physicians. Shortly after my acupuncture training I was introduced to the elemental mysteries of Earth, Water, Air and Fire through Lisa Michaels and the *Natural Rhythms Institute*[3.] I have chosen to meld her teachings with my own studies of acupuncture and Eastern medicine. My perspective on women's health, then, has become deeper and richer than my initial Western training.

This chapter is all about cycles and their role in health and wellness. Since menstrual cycles are the basis of our health as women, I'll explore the hormonal symphony of the menstrual cycle and add my perspectives on the elemental teachings of each phase of the cycle. Hormonal balance will be the overall focus with a look at three situations where balance is off: in infertility, PMS, and menopausal symptoms. My goal will be to list out tools for you for restoring balance and embracing life so it can be long, strong, sexy, and fun!

Lifestyle Choices and Health

The US Department of Health and Human Services gathers data on life expectancy every year. Since 1970, our life expectancy as women has risen from 75 to almost 81 years although racial and income discrepancies persist. The most common causes of death for women (in order) are heart disease, stroke, lung cancer, chronic lung disease, Alzheimer's, accidents/injuries, breast cancer, influenza, and colon cancer. What if I told you that **three** lifestyle habits or choices would prevent 80% of the heart disease and stroke, 80% of the type 2 diabetes and 40% of the cancers? Although it seems unbelievable, it's true. The CDC estimates that 1) following a healthy diet, 2) taking up a regular exercise program and 3) not smoking can make a huge impact on how long we live.

Perhaps just as important as living a long life is choosing to live with purpose, verve, and consciousness. I believe this is best done by connecting to the cycle of life, our menstrual cycles and the incredible hormonal symphony that unfolds each month between our endocrine organs. Using hormones as chemical messengers, our body prepares monthly for reproduction. My training as an Ob/Gyn labeled this the hypothalamic-pituitary-ovarian axis, suggesting that the hypothalamus in the brain, the anterior portion of the pituitary, and the ovaries were the only players in this cycle. Obviously this isn't true! Our adrenals and their ability to guide us through stressful situations, our liver and kidneys and their role in clearing toxins from our bodies, and our thyroid and its connection to our metabolic rate are just three of the many ways we can change our menstrual cycle frequency or flow!

I am convinced that we need to also balance the anabolic hormones of the menstrual cycle (estrogen and progesterone) and the catabolic hormones of the adrenals (cortisol). It is through this balance that we can then explore ways to increase libido, improve fertility, decrease menstrual cramps, reduce the size of uterine fibroids, and ease menopausal symptoms. Rather than digging into the physiology and biochemistry, I'm drawn to explore the four segments of the menstrual cycle from an elemental point of view. In

34

this way, we can broaden our understanding without too much science and complexity. In the following sections, then, menstruation is represented by the water phase (emotional realm); the follicular or egg recruitment portion of the cycle is the air phase (the mental realm), ovulation and implantation is the fire phase (action realm); and the luteal portion of the cycle is the earth phase (the physical realm).

The Menstrual Cycle—Water

So let's begin with menstruation and its connection to the Water phase of the cycle. Our body begins menstrual bleeding in response to a drop in the hormones estrogen and progesterone after ovulation or egg release. The lining of the uterus (endometrium) has built up and thickened in preparation for pregnancy and implantation. If no pregnancy occurs, the hormone levels drop and the lining starts to break down and flow out. Menstrual blood consists of the top layer of the endometrium and the blood that is contained in the blood vessels within it. If the layer has built up thickly in response to high doses of hormones such as estrogen, the flow is heavier. The length and volume of blood flow is related to how thick the lining of endometrium has developed and how rapidly hormone levels drop after ovulation.

In the context of menstruation, I have seen many women hold on to the fear, anger, and frustration that came with puberty and the onset of their menstrual cycles. Almost always this has been because they were either unprepared for puberty and the normal changes in their bodies or because they were prepared poorly by an older sister, a mother, or an aunt. Their family either avoided the discussion entirely or painted the picture of menstrual cycles as dirty or painful and the prophecy was fulfilled! Water carries with it the emotional charge of life experiences and stories, and has the capacity to flow or settle depending on the energetic container.

Our culture adds to these negative menstrual feelings with commercials heralding contraceptive options that limit the number of cycles each year. And, of course, my medical training approached menstrual complaints with the narrow focus of two options: surgical or hormonal therapy. We Ob/Gyn physicians were taught to recommend either removing the uterus (hysterectomy) or scraping or burning out the endometrium (D&C or laser or thermal ablation) if childbearing is completed. Birth control pills, shots, rings, or IUD's were recommended if childbearing is not completed. I had very little exposure to integrative approaches to abnormal menstrual bleeding.

One of my recent teachers, Lewis Mehl-Medrona, MD, PhD, recently shared the concept of *nogi*, which means "way of being" in the language of the indigenous Lakota Indians. The Lakota believed our nogi is a combination of every story that ever influenced us—whether through our own self-talk or through another person. They believe that healing is possible when bad or painful stories are replaced with good stories. I've had the honor of helping many women reframe and reclaim their menstrual stories during my medical career to date. In addition, I saw many women clear these stories from their consciousness through their work with *Natural Rhythms* and the *Priestess Process*™4.

Emotional health, then, or a clear, clean flow of the element Water is the key component of the menstrual portion of the cycle. Water energy requires constant awareness of what is "muddying" our field of energy. Our relationships need to be clear, clean and current. Our emotional connection to our work, our home, and our family needs to be "washed" frequently and cleared as needed. Like most elemental forces, Water needs to be flowing to avoid becoming stagnant. Tools to clear Water energy include a consistent practice such as journaling daily or a gratitude list. Counseling is another option. Breath work, meditation, yoga and prayer are also tools for clearing the emotional phase of the cycle.

The Follicular Phase—Air

The second stage of the menstrual cycle is the follicular phase, in which the hormone estrogen tells the lining of the uterus to re-grow and start to thicken. There is also "recruitment" of an egg in the ovaries, as one of the many follicles containing a small egg is encouraged to grow and prepare for release (ovulation).

The follicular phase of the menstrual cycle is best represented by the element of Air. The mental realm steps up—exploring the idea of conception. A woman consciously considers either growing a family, using contraception, or avoiding sex during ovulation. Much like the delivering mother I mentioned in the start of the chapter, she is considering the impact of a new life in her world. What would it mean to her marriage or to her family? The element of Air allows ideas to shift and shimmer, organizing and planning and considering all angles of a situation.

We don't always allow Air to work its magic in our lives. We "react" to life rather than consciously choosing direction and focus. The element Air can represent new ideas and perspectives that "blow" in to life's situations that watery emotions have allowed to stagnate. I like to encourage my clients to encourage Air by using "vision board" collages with ideas that have come to them through their meditation or journaling. It may be a picture of a home or a baby or a life mate or financial security. By consciously choosing a direction and focusing our intentions we allow Air to flow in and through us.

Ovulation and Ejaculation—Fire

The third phase of the cycle is ovulation. It is during this phase that the recruited egg releases an enzyme that works on the surface of the ovary to allow it to dissolve and allows the egg to be released. Soft finger-like projections on the ends of the fallopian tube called fimbria capture the egg through a combination of movement and chemical cues and angle it down the tube to the uterine cavity. By this time, the lining of the uterus is thick and ready for implantation. If a man's sperm is in the vagina during this time, the sperm swim up through the cervix, the opening of the uterus, and meet the egg in the fallopian tube. Once a sperm penetrates the outer layer of the egg, fertilization occurs and the fertilized egg then travels to the uterus and implants. The element Fire best represents this phase of the cycle. Fire represents the action realm and this phase is all about action! The egg inside the ovary is acting on the ovary for release, the sperm are swimming, the fimbria are moving, and the fertilized egg is implanting.

Fire is absolutely essential in our lives. Fire represents ideas and activities that stretch our brains and bodies such as painting, dancing or singing. We use Fire energy to design a menu for our family or to create scrapbook vacation memories. We also know that Fire as an element has to be contained, controlled, and nourished. Forest fires are good examples of

Fire out of control. In the context of our cycles, fertility drugs are examples of medicines that stimulate Fire. They are monitored closely to prevent too many ovulation follicles (and too many fertilized eggs) since carrying more than twins can significantly increase the risk of premature labor and birth.

The Luteal Phase—Earth

The fourth and final phase of the cycle is the luteal phase. This is the portion of the cycle after ovulation when the lining of the uterus supports the implanted and fertilized egg. The ovarian follicle that released the egg re-forms to make a yellowish structure called the "corpus luteum". This is Latin for "yellow body" because it appears yellow under the microscope. The corpus luteum releases progesterone, a hormone that supports the lining of the uterus during implantation and the early developing fertilized egg.

The luteal phase is best represented by the element of Earth. Earth is the element of nourishment and connection. Earth allows us to appreciate and honor our physical bodies as the conscious connection to our creation. Earth represents the nourishing ovary that releases hormones. Earth is also the uterus nourishing the implanted egg and encouraging growth and development. Too much sugar or alcohol are just two examples of how metabolism can be affected and impact our Earth energy. We acknowledge Earth when we nourish ourselves with healthy food, with healthy breath, with healthy thoughts, and with healthy relationships.

Reproduction is not possible without a balance between each of the elements. The element Water is essential to the emotional component of the menstrual phase. The element Air is essential to the mental component of the follicular phase. The element Fire is essential to the action component of the ovulation phase. And finally, the element Earth is essential to the physical component of the luteal phase. Loss or imbalance of any one of these elements results in an irregular or anovulatory (no ovulation) cycle. The gift of co-creation is Spirit moving in and through us as the balanced elemental energies work their magic.

The Elements and Fertility

So let's put the elements in context for a few examples now. First, consider a couple that is planning a family. Ideally, they discuss their plans with a physician or midwife and review their medical histories. Are they on medications that affect any of the elements? Examples could be hypertension drugs that interfere with a man's erection (the element Fire) or migraine or epilepsy drugs that could interfere with early implantation (the element Earth). They review all prescription drugs, vitamins, supplements, toxic exposures at work, etc. and start 400mcg of folic acid and 1 to 2 grams of high quality fish oil daily to reduce the incidence of birth defects and to improve the baby's brain development. She is vaccinated for rubella (German measles) at least three months prior to pregnancy if her titer is low and they are both given a physical exam for routine age-appropriate health screening. They are guided towards nutritional choices that include a wide variety of colorful vegetables, lean protein and whole grains. They are told to avoid alcohol, recreational drugs, excessive caffeine, artificial sweeteners, and sugar. They are encouraged to exercise together three times a week and look at life balance issues between home and work before attempting pregnancy. Parenting styles and personal stories are shared. Religious and spiritual discussions are held. They are encouraged to review together their plans on breastfeeding, work schedule adjustments, early childhood education, corporal punishment, etc. Once they are ready to attempt pregnancy, they honor each phase of the menstrual cycle as it occurs and connect to the elements together and separately. Connection to co-creation and elemental teachings isn't part of most people's pre-conception planning, but I believe it should be!

Now in contrast, let me give you a patient story. I'll call her Jane (not her real name). She and her husband John had been trying for pregnancy for a year. She went straight to IVF (in vitro fertilization) after failing to get pregnant with three cycles of Clomid™ (clomiphene citrate—an oral drug that stimulates egg release). The IVF cycle failed, and Jane is in my office to add acupuncture to her next IVF cycle because data has shown that IVF pregnancy rates are higher with acupuncture. She's working in the tech field as a manager and works 50+ hours a week. She hasn't planned a post-pregnancy work schedule; she figures she'll "deal with that during the pregnancy". John travels 50% of the time for his job and they are threatening lay-offs. She drinks four cups of coffee a day and eats carryout food almost daily. Prior to starting the Clomid™ she was on the pill for the last fifteen years—she started it as a teenager because her cramps were "horrible". Jane feels stressed and anxious because pregnancy hasn't come to her immediately. Everything else in her life came with hard work and study. Her physician has classified her infertility as "unexplained" and that makes her feel helpless and frustrated.

Jane spent the first appointment in my office learning how to breathe and how to eat. Acupuncture is based on balancing and tapping in to life force energy or "qi". Qi is represented by a Chinese symbol with one component for vapor or air (often interpreted to mean Spirit) and one component for rice. The ancient Chinese believed that we feed our life force by the quality of our breath and connection to Spirit along with the quality of our diet.

Jane and I reviewed nutrition thoroughly and mapped out a strategy for easy nutritious meals. We also spent five or ten minutes learning a relaxation practice based just on the breath. We discussed each phase of the menstrual cycle and developed a set of affirmations for her to use at least once a day throughout the cycle. I encouraged Jane to "book" appointments with John to either walk around their neighborhood or cook a meal together three or four times a week. I asked that they each write a "lover's list" of five to ten things that they loved about each other and share a few of the items on the list each day. We scheduled acupuncture every two weeks until her IVF cycle and then did a treatment with her stimulation drugs, with her egg retrieval, and with her embryo transfer. She called to let me know the pregnancy test was positive and assured me she'd keep up the breath work, nutrition, and couple time with John.

From an elemental point of view, Jane needed Earth and Water to successfully conceive. She needed to tap into feelings about her cycles and honor their release rather than resenting the pain and her perception of the failure of conception. She could also apply a more mindful approach to her nutrition by consciously stepping in to the awareness of co-creation and acknowledging the needs of her own life-force energy and also the needs of the potential new life she was inviting into her body.

The Elements and PMS

What about premenstrual syndrome or PMS? PMS is the cyclic occurrence of physical and emotional symptoms prior to the menstrual cycle. Symptoms vary from woman to woman but can include abdominal bloating, headaches, skin acne, irritability, weepiness, and easy anger. My Western training gave me two options for clients with PMS: the birth control pill or an anti-depressant. The birth control pill helps to decrease cramps and the amount of menstrual flow if either of those physical symptoms are an issue. The anti-depressant blunts the emotional symptoms of PMS.

Similar to the elemental approach for fertility, PMS responds well to the same integrative approach. In addition to exploring breath work, optimal nutrition, and the elemental phases of the menstrual cycle, I also introduce the Wheel of the Year. In our northern hemisphere the days are shorter and darker in the winter as the earth finishes its harvests and rests. After the Winter Solstice, the days start to lengthen and the growing cycle begins for the next year. Women in our culture often have a "foot on the gas pedal" constantly as they work, care for a home, and volunteer at church or in the community. This is unbalanced Fire without the containment of Earth and Water. There is no conscious slowing or easing of responsibilities. There is no darkness or quiet or "recharging" for the next cycle (or day or week). As a matter of fact, the workweek is usually peppered with early morning or after work meetings or exercise classes. Add in a child's soccer practice and game schedule or piano lessons or school assignments. Or on top of all that, add concerns for aging parents or marriage difficulties. Is the picture coming clear for you?

PMS is always worsened by fatigue and responds well to practices like meditation, breath work, or yoga. A mindful approach to nutrition can also help the symptoms. Cravings for chocolate or salty foods, for example, are signs of imbalance. Most of us need more "down time" written into our schedules. What if instead of checking Facebook or watching television, the time was spent meditating or in prayer? We are constantly in contact by texting, phone calls, and emails. I suggest an enforced quiet time daily, even if it's only 15 minutes twice a day.

The Elements and Menopause

With most of us living to our 80's, we spend at least a third of our lives in menopause. Our fertility gradually wanes and the cycle of life changes so that both the follicular phase (egg recruitment) and the ovulation phase (egg release) decreases and then stops. This corresponds to less Air and Fire in the cycle, leaving only Water and Earth. Not surprisingly, most women complain of mental fogginess and fatigue and sluggishness as they approach menopause. Their sleep is disrupted by hot flashes and night sweats. The promise of hormone therapy (my training referred to it as "hormone **replacement** therapy") has been shown to have attendant risks such as blood clots and an increased incidence of breast cancer. If hormones aren't used, the recommendation (again!) is anti-depressants for hot flashes. This discussion is beyond the scope of this chapter, but suffice it to say that the Western approach to menopause and aging is inadequate and potentially dangerous.

Asian and Native American cultures revere the elderly and honor their teachings and listen to their stories. In contrast, we have so few role models for aging with grace and balance. We are in a youth-focused culture with blatant biases and fears about aging and death. Plastic surgery and hair dye are commonly used to remove wrinkles or grey hair. Our aging parents and grandparents are often isolated from our lives with brief glimpses at holidays or special occasions.

Reframing menopause with an elemental approach allows us to acknowledge the shift from reproductive Air and Fire to postmenopausal Air and Fire as ovulation decreases and gradually stops. Most of us hit menopause as our children are teenagers or young adults. Our nurturing is changing shape and dynamics. Rather than nourishing the potential spark of life in an egg each month, we look outside our body to nourish something else. I've seen menopausal women nourish a new business or non-profit. I've seen them start a new career. I've seen them nourish an art or music therapy program at a hospital. My clients have taken up new hobbies such as painting or classes in mediation during their menopausal years. Freedom from nurturing within the family allows them to nurture outside in their worlds.

Like my clients above, adding Air during the menopausal years corresponds to stimulating our brain with classes or books or new experiences. We add Fire to our menopausal years by moving. We may choose to move off the couch in front of the TV and away from the computer monitor. Perhaps it's an exercise or dance classes. Perhaps it's dancing in our living room in our socks in the morning.

Although our cultural expectation of aging is loss of function and dwindling towards death, I encourage my clients to look at their own *nogi*, or summary of stories, and make sure that they are choosing their truth rather than some one else's perception of what aging looks like.

An elemental approach to women's health underlies the basis of our physical health. Our physical health is closely tied to our emotional, mental, and spiritual health. As we nourish our physical body, we tend our own physical temple and prepare to celebrate the gift of the days we are given.

About Claudia Harsh MD

Dr Claudia Harsh MD is an integrative gynecologist and physician acupuncturist currently working at Living Well Health & Wellness Center in Dallas, Texas. She is the author of the recently published book "*Finding Grace and Balance in the Cycle of Life: Exploring Integrative Gynecology*" and has completed the two-year fellowship in Integrative Medicine through the University of Arizona. She has a strong interest in a holistic approach to women's health. She works with her clients on breath work, biofeedback, nutrition, vitamins and nutrition supplements, acupuncture, and frequency specific microcurrent. Her passion is that her clients achieve optimal emotional, mental, physical, and spiritual health.

Chapter 5

Cutting the Cords of Shame to Reclaim Your Passion

Helen Magers LPCC

Shame forged the emotional core of my childhood. I am a product of the baby-boomer generation. I grew up on a small farm in Kentucky with three sisters and parents who were overwhelmed with work and worry. My parents grew up during the Great Depression, and like many others of that generation had neither the time nor energy to reflect on the emotional well-being of their children. Providing food and clothing for the children were the priorities.

My mother controlled me and my sisters by telling us that we "should be ashamed" when we made a mistake, broke a family rule, or deliberately did something we knew we should not have done. The sense of shame caused us to be quiet and compliant which is what she needed in order to manage all her daily duties.

A cord of shame quietly wrapped itself around my sense of self as I attended school. I idolized and feared my teachers. I believed teachers knew everything so when my third grade teacher told me I could not do math I believed her. What I heard in my 8 year old mind was that I was stupid and unable to learn anything, especially math.

Shame was so much part of my life as a young girl. I was taller than anyone in my elementary school classes and physically developed earlier than my friends. I spent my middle school years slumped over so I would not seem so tall and to hide newly-formed breasts. As a pre-teen I was sent for ballroom dance classes. My height made it impossible to dance with boys; they were not as tall and naturally their faces were even with my chest, a source of shame. I was told to take the male role and dance with other girls and today I still try to lead when dancing.

The shame I felt as a child drew me to research how this emotion, which affects so many of us, is initiated. I learned that emotional cords are created whenever there is a strong, emotional connection with another individual. Negative cords can develop when we experience a sense of betrayal, blame, anger, or shame. Negative emotional cords can drain energy and keep us stuck in patterns of the past.

Shame, or the feeling of not being "enough", greatly affects the way we mature. Negative emotional cords, forged early in our lives by shame, become firmly attached to our psyche and can tie us up emotionally for years. We learn shame early in our lives but carry it with us like a silent, dark presence as we age.

Early childhood development research tells us that a child's first stage of development is to learn basic trust. The second stage is to experience shame and since we can only be shamed by someone we revere or respect, we take to heart what they may say to us. We take it in, internalize it, and believe it.

The belief that I was stupid and unable to learn followed me through young adulthood. When I graduated from high school no one suggested I go to college. That fact helped to reinforce the cord of shame I experienced about my inability to make good grades.

At 30 years old, I had the means to attend college but I was concerned the university would not accept me based on my poor performance in high school. My sister, in an effort to encourage me, reassured me that universities were anxious to provide services to "older returning students".

Although I made good grades, my mind swirled with thoughts of being discovered a fraud and being asked to leave. Even when I graduated with my Bachelor's Degree, Summa Cum Laude, I refused to believe it was because I was smart. I felt I had cleverly fooled all my professors. Graduate school success helped to loosen the shame cord slightly but self-doubt was still a constant companion.

It was not until much later in life that I began the work of dismantling the negative emotional cords of shame that held me hostage. Psychological counseling helped, as did my introduction to *Natural Rhythms*. Learning the power of the elemental forces to heal and make one whole was the beginning of a new way of coping with shame.

Nature provides us with incredible power sources: Earth, Air, Water, Fire and Spirit are all available to us if we "tune in" to their energy. Using the healing power of the natural world I began to work through the memories, thoughts, and feelings that kept me trapped in shame. Learning to tune in and take advantage of Nature's gifts is one of the most extraordinary events in my life.

I began my journey by setting a solid foundation in Earth, the physical realm of nature. The physical grounding power of Earth allowed me to create a container to hold my essence while I explored the events that shaped the energetic cords of shame in my life. Earth taught me to be slow and careful, and to take things one step at a time in order to realize my purpose.

The patience of Earth can be seen in the turning of the seasons. There is a time to lay fallow, a time of awakening, a time of growth, and a time to harvest. The Wheel of the Year taught me to slow down, to take stock of my thoughts and feelings, and to be gentle with myself when feeling overwhelmed.

Using the support of Earth, I wrote my "story" and by doing so I explored the memories, thoughts, and feelings that created the cords of shame. Writing and reading my story aloud helped to "ground" my experience, and sharing my story with a circle of sisters enhanced the support and made my feelings legitimate.

The exercise of writing and investigating the "roots" of the cords provided me the opportunity to recognize them and to begin to understand some of my emotional reactions to events. I can now stop, examine my feelings, remember how the feelings were formed, and make a mature choice on how to deal with them. I cannot claim to never experience the feeling of shame but my understanding of where the feelings originate helps to reduce emotional discomfort.

As I continued to explore the origin of my feelings of shame I recognized how deeply the emotional experience was. Writing and reading my story resulted in many tears, and as I allowed the tears to flow I began to realize how much better I felt after a "good cry". Water is the emotional realm of nature and is a basic necessity of life. We cannot physically live without Water and, as I discovered, we cannot heal emotionally without tears.

Growing up, my sisters and I hadn't been encouraged to express strong emotions of any kind, especially sadness. Each of us cried privately when our grandparents and parents died. We hid our tears from one another and grieved alone. Crying in front of people was a new experience for me as I journeyed through the natural elements. And I let the tears flow.

Discovering the therapeutic power of Water helped me to come to grips with the pain I had experienced because of shame. It taught me there was nothing to be embarrassed about when strong feelings bubbled up and tears filled my eyes. Allowing the Water to move through my body was cleansing and refreshing.

I have always appreciated the sound of Water, the sound of waves lapping against the shore and the trickle of small stream. Both are restful and refreshing. Anytime I can experience the calmness of a body of water I immerse my "soul" in this powerful natural element.

I remember, as a twelve year old, being baptized. In the Baptist Church you are literally dipped into a pool of water to "wash away your sins". This is how I see the power of Water in my life now. It helps to wash away the sadness and shame; it soothes and calms me, and I don't hesitate to use it to enrich my life.

As I continued my work of disengaging the cords of shame, I was introduced to the power of Air. Air is the mental realm of the elemental forces and, of course, our thoughts are frequently the source of our discomfort or unhappiness.

The feelings of shame I harbored were formed by thoughts, and I learned through working with the element of Air that I needed to listen to my inner voice of reason. Listening, internalizing, and believing negative messages from those outside myself helped to create the shame I felt. The realization that I was at a point in my life when I could choose the messages I wished to recognize was incredibly empowering.

From Air I realized I could choose to stay stuck in shame or I could move to a higher frequency. I could stay afraid and earth-bound or I could fly. I could continue to blame my "failures" on others, or I could take responsibility for mistakes and move forward with a commitment to do better the next time.

This was an incredibly powerful time for me. I had not realized how tightly the cords of shame had bound me to a belief that I was unworthy but now I was able to identify my strengths and to acknowledge my weaknesses without feeling I had little value.

My experience working with the element of Air taught me to set an intention each day—to set in my mind a goal to be reached that day. I have created the habit of setting a daily intention before I get out of bed and try to keep it in mind throughout the day. There are days when I am able to reach the goal and others when I am not. But when I do not reach the goal I refuse to fall back into the "shame/blame game". I realize tomorrow is another day and I have the opportunity to work on it again.

Air is the natural element that truly keeps us alive. Think of the times someone has told you to stop and "take a deep breath". Taking a deep breath calms us and helps us to think clearly. I was told so often in my life to "slow down" and I now know the message was to stop, breathe, and think clear thoughts. My regret of learning this lesson so late in my life was quickly replaced with my gratitude of having received this gift from the natural world.

By this point in my journey my freedom from the cords of shame had been absolutely life changing. I grounded myself by writing and sharing my story, I recognized it was okay to show deep emotional feelings, and I discovered the power of slowing down, breathing deeply, and listening to my inner voice. The next step was as natural as Nature itself: Fire, the action needed to cut the cords of shame.

The natural element of Fire brings us warmth, energy, and is necessary to sustain life. Crops grow, trees blossom, and the world flourishes because of the warmth of the sun. We need Fire and action if we are going to grow and thrive. The gifts of learning from the other elemental forces helped me to consider the best way to use the assistance of Fire and action in my desire to be free of the cords of shame.

My first inclination was to take action by ripping those negative feelings out and throwing them as far away as possible. I wanted to be finished with this. I was tired of having these old feelings of shame haunt me. I then considered how long these cords had been part of my life and my belief system. They were part of me and I could not think how I would just throw them in the trash. After shedding some healing tears I told them I no longer needed them. I wanted them to know I now recognized how they were forged and it was time they went away and were no longer part of me.

I decided to create a physical representation of my cords. Using a variety of art media, I produced a concrete symbol of my feelings of shame—of not being "enough".

I took a deep breath and struck a match, placed it on the "cords" letting the fire curl and char the paper until I dropped it into a bowl. Looking at the ash that was left I wondered how I had allowed shame to color so much of my life, but then I realized there is no shame in shame. It is something we all share and constantly have to work to control. The simple act of burning my paper shame cords was not a magic trick that quickly ended my feelings of shame. They creep back occasionally, trying to regain a foothold in my psyche. I have to be vigilant, stay grounded, be aware of and accept my feelings, then breathe deeply, and take some action in order to keep them at bay.

Spirit is what helps me stay on top of those feelings. Spirit is what I go to each morning when I set my intention for the day. It is what sustains me and helps me with the work of becoming a meaningful member of society.

Spirit is the creator of the elemental forces and reminds us of the Divine source of all power.

As a child, I was taken to church, it seemed, every time the church door opened. I was confused by the idea of a loving God who was punishing and would send you straight to Hell if you messed up. All the church leaders were men, and there were few female role models in the Bible for a young girl. Men seemed to be in charge of religion and women worked in the church kitchen fixing food for the congregation. This arrangement made me think that God did not like women. Religion was confusing and so I stopped going to church and shut God and religion out of my life.

Because I attended a Catholic university I had to take a certain number of class hours in religion. A professor who happened to be a nun remarked that all the qualities we apply to Jesus are feminine qualities: kindness, loving, forgiving, gentleness, etc. Wow! I remember thinking, "Could there be a feminine part to God?" What a thought.

When I found *Natural Rhythms*, I discovered the God/Goddess belief in the Divine and I knew I had found what I had been searching for all these years. It was here I learned the feminine and masculine parts of the Divine. I was delighted to know both parts of the Divine are to be acknowledged and honored, and in honoring both I feel more connected to the Divine, more able to turn to Spirit for guidance.

Spirit helped me to recognize the need to rid myself of the shame that was holding me back from experiencing all life to the fullest. Spirit helped me to ground that purpose in the physical world, bless it with my tears, bring clear thinking and my inner resources to the task in order to formulate the action needed to fulfill my purpose. What a lovely design! Everything I needed in the natural world connected by Spirit.

Spirit helped me to remove the cords of shame gently, with love. Spirit also helped me remove them at the root rather than simply cut them off; to thank them for being part of my life because their presence helped create the woman I am today; to let them go; and to recognize that they have left a mark that must be cared for daily.

I began the journey by tuning into the gifts of Nature and I recognize the importance of working through each of the elemental forces to reach a level of understanding that will allow me to prosper. Playwright Oscar Wilde once said, "To love oneself is the beginning of a life-long romance". My work with the elements was that beginning for me.

As a psychotherapist I work with men and women who are struggling with overwhelming feelings of shame. I have used the elemental forces in my work to help them examine the thoughts and feelings that fashioned their cords of shame. I have found many of them willing to engage in the elemental journey even when they do not quite understand how the natural world can help them overcome feelings of shame.

In addition to my private practice, I work with women who have been found guilty of drug and prostitution charges and sentenced to complete a drug treatment program. This population is often so saturated in shame they initially require some encouragement to begin looking at how shame has shaped their lives.

It has been my experience these women are reluctant to imagine they are capable of change or to imagine a brighter future. So often they get stuck looking back at their failures they find it difficult to look ahead and plan for a positive future. Frequently they have promised parents, partners, and children that the treatment will work this time, only to fall back into old habits and behaviors once they leave the treatment center. Sadly, they believe everyone they love has given up on them, and frequently they are correct.

One young woman told me she was not interested in planning a future. She had disappointed her parents, husband, and children so many times they could no longer believed her promises to stay "clean", so she knew no reason to get her hopes up that things would be different this time. Soon after our conversation, she participated in a group session I facilitated on the solid foundation of the Earthly realm. We talked about how the Earth provides us with abundance and provides solid support for us.

Each woman was asked to stand, shut her eyes, and feel the support of the Earth under her feet. I asked the group members to feel the energy of Mother Earth and imagine that energy coming up through the floor, into their feet, and then flowing through their body all the way to their finger tips. I asked each woman to write her feelings about the Earth exercise in a journal that would become her blueprint for how to use the power of Earth to help her reach her potential.

I was amazed at how quickly most of the women understood the power of the Earthly realm and tapped into Her support. The woman who claimed she could not dream of a future wrote that she felt uncomfortable at first but began to feel peaceful as she stood there. She stated she liked the feeling of "the Earth giving me, of all people, some love" and the possibility of some source of energy outside herself.

I saw her several days later standing in the dayroom, eyes shut and arms extended, recapturing the warm, peaceful feeling she felt that day in group. She told me she returned to this exercise whenever she felt overwhelmed and claimed it calmed her. She struggled with the journal writing but eventually she was able to write and even draw some pictures that represented what she hoped would be her future.

As I worked with the women, I heard and witnessed their frustration of living with fifty other women. Patience was generally on short supply but there was an abundance of gossip and rumors. I noticed that often a woman would react to a situation in a verbally abusive manner and then experience shame about her loss of control. I thought that perhaps the element of Air could assist them.

We started with learning some stress tolerance skills, such as counting to ten before responding or physically retreating from the situation in order to breathe deeply and regain their composure. We also learned square breathing. Square breathing required them to breathe in to the count of four, hold the breath for four counts, and then release the breath to the count of four. They would repeat that four times.

As we practiced square breathing the women were able to understand that Air was giving them the gift of time: time to **think** before responding. They learned Air is the mental realm, and as we breathe deeply our bodies fill with oxygen and increase our ability to think clearly. Thinking clearly can help to lessen any negative reaction and increase positive ones.

One woman made me laugh one day by telling me she had overheard another woman talking about her. She started to react by "telling her off", but then took herself to a quiet corner and did the square breathing exercise. But after completing the exercise, she was convinced she still wanted "to tell her off" and did so in a non-violent, verbally appropriate manner. I complimented her on her restraint and assured her that square breathing would not take away all angry feelings, but would allow her the luxury of time to make sure she would get her point across while not escalating the tension of the moment.

Thinking through a problem is difficult for men and women who have been degraded and criticized most of their lives. Their sense of shame is so entrenched they are compelled to create seemingly impenetrable defenses and immediately strike back when they believe they have been "disrespected". But a defensive attitude keeps most people at bay and only deepens their isolation. Understanding how to use the power of Air, to use breath and to allow them the time to think things through can help to dismantle the overwhelming feelings of shame.

Each of us experiences shame differently. My shame cords were forged out of feelings of not being good enough, not being smart enough. Others may recognize their shame was generated by their poor decisions. Men and women who have experienced sexual and/or physical abuse as children often experience shame since they so frequently blame themselves for the abuse. Understanding how shame is created in your life is the beginning of a journey that will ultimately enrich your life and give you the power and energy to create the life of your dreams.

How can you use Nature's elemental forces as a system to clear old shame baggage? There are five steps I recommend to begin the process:

- Start by grounding yourself in the power of Earth. Create a harmonious, safe place in your home, pay attention to your body, and gratefully acknowledge the gifts of Earth. Once you feel as though you are grounded, begin to write the memories of where the cords of shame originated. Be still, lie fallow, and let the seeds of rational thought help you begin to clear the cords of shame.

- Clear the emotions that may come from your examination of old shame messages by tapping into the power of Water. Ask friends and family for the emotional support you may feel you need during this time. Be willing to accept the gifts of friendship and the joy of giving as well as receiving. Life ebbs and flows; you may feel totally complete one day and the next feel ready to give up because you are overwhelmed. Remember, every ocean wave rises and falls. Learn to "ride the wave"; hang on at the peak when emotions are high then land clean, clear, and current, ready to let Water wash over you with its healing power. Stand in the shower and visualize the feelings of shame swirling down the drain!

- Thoughts are where the shame cords originate so it is natural that Air be part of your journey. Too often we can confuse feelings with thoughts since one closely follows the other, therefore clarity of thought is important. Knowing whether your memories are accurate and keeping in mind your perspective at the time the memory was formed are most important. You may find that the shame cord was forged from poor communication, a misunderstanding, or was not ever true. As you write your memories, check the validity of the thoughts. Were you an eight year old hearing she was stupid or was it a student with a teacher who was having a bad day?

- When you feel ready to take action, let Fire provides the energy needed to take apart and remove the cords of shame. Fire is about passion, movement, and joy. Put some music on and move! Visualize the gentle loosening of the cords and ask that they leave so you can grow to the next phase of existence.

- Praying, meditating, journal keeping, and researching all the "roots" of your shame cords may be an exhausting exercise, but the Divine Masculine and Feminine are prepared to embrace you in love and compassion. Turning to Spirit for guidance is as easy as sitting quietly and listening to your inner voice. The poet Anne Sexton advised us to "Put your ear down next to your soul and listen hard"[4] is there to give you what you need if you "listen hard".

All these suggestions will help you begin the work of clearing negative shame cords. For additional information on workshops available, go to my web-site: www.helenmagers.com

About Helen Magers LPCC

Helen has devoted herself to helping those who suffer with feelings of shame and guilt. She is passionate about her work and committed to providing assistance to those who suffer low self-esteem and self-respect. Helen helps individuals and group members to discover their authentic voice by using Nature's elemental forces. She calls on her own struggle with shame to model a path to emotional wellness. Helen is a Licensed Clinical Counselor trained in Gestalt Therapy, Eye Movement Desensitization and Reprocessing (EMDR) therapy, and has earned Expert Status through the Natural Rhythms Institute.

Chapter 6

5 Minutes a Day To Bring Your Dreams Into Reality

Tammy Huber-Wilkins MD

Our deepest fear is not that we are inadequate.
Our deepest fear is that we are powerful beyond measure.
It is our light, not our darkness, that most frightens us.
We ask ourselves, who am I to be brilliant, gorgeous, talented and
fabulous?
Actually, who are you not to be?
You are a child of God. Your playing small doesn't serve the world.
There is nothing enlightened about shrinking so that other people will
not feel insecure around you.

We were born to manifest the glory of God that is within us.
It is not in just some of us. It is in everyone.
And as we let our own light shine, we unconsciously give
people permission to do the same.

As we are liberated from our own fear, our presence automatically
liberates others.

Marianne Williamson [1]

The key to manifesting your dreams with just 5 minutes a day is to know what to do in those 5 minutes. This chapter is a guide on how to utilize the power that is already within you and how to get clear on what it is that you really want. I end the chapter by sharing my stories of how I used this technique to manifest a husband and then a baby in my 40's.

My experience of life is that we are not taught that we are powerful manifestors. We are not taught that we can make anything happen in our lives with clear intention. When little kids have "grandiose" beliefs about their abilities, we call it magical thinking and laugh at their innocence. I believe that the minds of those children have not yet been brain washed to think small or to be filled with fear about all the things that can go wrong in life. When we observe great things happen or when people overcome great adversity, we see it as luck or a fluke, or something that happens to somebody else but not us. I have always been mesmerized by the stories of how Olympians overcame adversity to make their dreams come true. Those stories are my favorite part of watching the Olympics because it awakens a knowing in me that we can all accomplish great things by staying focused and maintaining a belief that our dream will come true.

Thanks to Lisa Michaels and her *Natural Rhythms*™ program I have been reminded of my own ability to have whatever I desire. We ALL have this ability. As Marianne Williamson says so eloquently, "we are all a child of God." I use the term God/Goddess instead of God because many of us have been taught that God is masculine. At some level this gives the message that being feminine is not God-like. Everything in nature, including humans, carries feminine and masculine energy. We are all of the same matter; we are all equal; and we are all "powerful beyond measure".

Like many things in our lives, we tend to make things harder than they need to be. The 7 steps to bring our dreams into reality are actually quite simple:

1. Connect to your inner sacred self for clarity of desire. Be specific.
2. Set a time frame.
3. Create a 5 minute daily ceremony using the Elemental Forces.
4. Look and listen for clues and guidance.
5. Open to your dream showing up in a surprising way.
6. Connect to how it feels right now if your desire showed up this instant.
7. Offer gratitude and celebrate.

Connect to Your Inner Sacred Self for Clarity of Desire

The first step of being a powerful manifestor in your own life requires being quiet. Our lives have become chaotic and filled with technology and information overload. We are constantly given messages of how we should look, dress, act, spend our money, and live our lives. Many of us lose connection with our own inner voice, our intuition, our inner guidance system that tells us what brings us real joy, pleasure, and peace of mind. We are fooled into believing what the advertisers want us to believe about their products. The belief that we buy into is that looking a certain way, driving a particular type of car, living in a big house, having item XYZ is going to fill us up emotionally. It is quite silly if you look at it objectively, but these messages have become an ingrained part of our culture.

The first task for your daily 5 minutes is to write about what YOU really, really want for yourself. Allow yourself to get quiet and clear about why you have your desire and what you want to feel once you reach this desired goal.

It is important to be as specific as possible. Many times we ask God/Goddess for something without realizing we are being vague. God/Goddess only knows how to say YES. We are all familiar with the phrase: "Ask and it shall be given". What often happens is that our prayer was answered but we were not clear so we missed the response because the desire did not show up when and in the way we expected. This is how many of us have lost our belief in the power of our prayers.

I wish I had been offered a test or a class in high school or college about what makes me happy. Isn't it important to quiet all the "noise" in your life and connect to that deepest part of yourself to see what YOU are really passionate about? Somehow we expect that everyone will somehow figure this out but most of us never do. But it is never too late to get clear and be honest with yourself about the components of living the life your soul desires.

You may also find that your desire is not a tangible "thing" like a relationship, job, child, money, house, physical health, etc., but rather it is a state of mind. Perhaps you desire more happiness, success, or confidence. I suggest that you write or type the words of your desire so that you are clear and accurate about the request. You will need to state your desire clearly and succinctly in step three.

Set a Time Frame

Step two is to choose a time frame for when you want this desire to show up. Many of us, especially women, have been taught to be polite when we want something. You say something like "Dear God/Goddess, please bring me the man of my dreams—whenever you think I'm ready". You have just placed an order leaving it completely up to Spirit what type of man comes into your life and when. And then wonder why God/Goddess is not answering your prayers. Remember the premise here is that Spirit will only know the timing you desire if you set the timing.

Are you really ready for the man of your dreams to show up now? What are the SPECIFIC characteristics of this man? How prepared are you for that promotion or dream job to cross your path and what EXACTLY would that dream job look like? Set a time frame or be prepared to wait and perhaps miss the response to your request because God/Goddess chose the timing and you missed the signs. Know that the speed with which your desire arrives is up to you. If you don't really BELIEVE your desire can show up in the time frame you choose, then it won't. We will work on this in step 6 if you feel challenged with this step.

Create a 5 Minute Daily Ceremony Using the Elemental Forces

Step number three is to put all of your focus and attention on your desire for 5 minutes every day via a brief ceremony or prayer or meditation. You can put as much time as you want into this step but 5 minutes is the minimum. My experience is that I have more success with goals when they are brief and to the point. I set aside 5 minutes per day and occasionally spent 10-15 minutes per day when I called in my husband. When I use the word ceremony, I mean an often repeated action performed in accordance with a tradition of a set of rules. My definition of prayer is a conversation with God/Goddess or your Higher Power. And the word meditation describes a state of extreme relaxation and concentrated focus inward.

Your goal is to include in your prayer or ceremony something representing each of the Elemental Forces: Fire, Earth, Air, Water, and Spirit. This gives you all the components of creation. It is something that Lisa Michaels calls creating a unified field. Sometimes this process is referred to as the coagulation of the elements and Spirit. There is no right or wrong way to do this ceremony and there are a million options and combinations available to you. Everyone's ceremony or prayer will be unique to them and their desire. It's like making your favorite pie, you put in the ingredients that you enjoy and want. If you want to read more about creating ceremony and the Elemental Forces please refer to the book *Natural Rhythms*™ by Lisa Michaels, especially pages 207-228.

Examples of items that represent the Elemental Forces that could be used in your ceremony include:

Fire (the Action Realm)

Burning a candle or incense
Drumming
Movement or dance
Incorporating a picture of a dragon, snake, or lizard

Earth (the Physical Realm)

Items from Nature such as a rock, crystal, twig, or flower
Your body represents Earth so tune into it deeply
Gratitude
Any kind of body movement

Air (the Mental Realm)

Setting an intention through prayer or meditation
Music/Sound
Smell: flower essence or aromatic oil
Your conscious thought or visualization

Water (the Emotional Realm)

Placing water in a vase, bowl, or cup to honor it

A shell or other item related to water
Picture of a dolphin, whale, or fish
Feeling your emotions at the deepest level possible

Spirit (the Spiritual Realm)

Connecting to God/Goddess
Connecting to the Divine Masculine and Divine Feminine
Feel compassion for yourself and others
Connecting to and trusting your intuition or inner voice

Look and Listen for Clues and Guidance

The next step is to look and listen for clues or guidance from Spirit. For me, this is where the magic happens. I have had the most success with this step when I approach it with playfulness and anticipation of clues showing up frequently. Feeling this connection to Spirit has been very comforting and energizing. I approach it like a scavenger hunt where I am looking for clues and information that will take me to my requested desire. It might be something on TV or radio that you just happen to see or hear. It could be a comment from a stranger or overhearing something in someone else's conversation.

Be aware of what crosses your path once you start doing the ceremony. Please listen to your intuition even if you don't like the message. Trust that Spirit is leading you down a path to your desire. Spirit sometimes knows a path that we would never have thought of. Many times we don't listen to our intuition for one reason or another and then we miss out on the answered prayer. The process of your daily ceremony magnetizes your desire to you and synchronicities will start to happen.

Many of us learn to pray or connect with God/Goddess by observing others pray. But so often prayers are internal, and there is silence only if you are the observer. Many of us were taught repetitive prayer and have little experience communicating with Spirit in the same way we would talk to a good friend. I also wish I had gone to prayer class 101; this would have made life a little easier. Check in with yourself. Is it "okay" to ask for what you desire? Are there any blocking beliefs about what you are asking for? Do you really believe that all prayers are answered or that your prayer is valid? Will God/Goddess hear your prayer out of the bazillions of prayers that are sent out into the ethers every day? Do you sometimes put a loophole in your prayer that God/Goddess can have the final say in whether you "deserve" for your prayer to be answered?

God/Goddess didn't say "Ask and it shall be given IF you are really, really good". God/Goddess is waiting with a full heart to answer your prayers and to help you step into your best, most fulfilled, happiest, peaceful self. Ask away. Know that you are worthy and that you are a child of God. Say your prayer out loud if you are struggling at all with this step. Learn to speak to Spirit as you would your dearest and most trusted friend. This will help you speak from your heart and soul and be really clear about your desire.

Be sure you LISTEN to Spirit (your own intuition) for a response once you send out your prayer. Sometimes you will get an immediate response, an inner knowing or a sign of some type. Sometimes it will be days or weeks or longer before a clue shows up from Spirit. Often guidance from Spirit will come in your dreamtime. If you find yourself impatient, include a time frame in which you want to get a response. I always request that my clues and guidance from Spirit be obvious. I don't want subtle clues that I might miss. I encourage you to ask for clear assistance and pay attention to your own resistance.

Resistance is probably one of the biggest things that will take us out of the path of manifesting our desires and we often don't realize we are doing it. Resistance is when your intuition tells you to do something but you ignore it or rationalize why you should not follow your intuition. If you notice resistance or if you want to put more energy into this step of manifesting I suggest you make a vision board or collage that represents your desire. Notice your inner dialogue and belief system as you look for images and words that capture what you are trying to manifest for yourself. Do you feel confident and have an inner knowing that God/Goddess is working on your behalf to bring your dreams into reality? Or, do you find yourself struggling to find images or words because a part of you is skeptical that your dreams really can come true? You don't feel worthy or you perhaps are not sure what you really want. Keep the vision board somewhere that you will see it each day and consider including it in your daily ceremony.

When I was doing daily ceremony to draw into my life the man who would become my husband, I danced with mine as though I was dancing at my own wedding.

Open to Your Dream Showing up in a Surprising Way

Step number five speaks to opening yourself to the idea that you have no idea how Spirit may bring you exactly what you desire. Without realizing it, we often carry a specific image or belief in our mind about how our dreams are going to manifest. This can be another reason we miss Spirit's response. I received a powerful lesson about this when I asked Spirit for a baby at age 44. Trust that God/Goddess has some creative ways for our dreams to manifest, particularly when we put ourselves on the fast track. For example, if we asked God/Goddess to get us from Los Angeles to NYC there are a million paths from LA to NYC. Do you want to ride a bike or fly non-stop? Do you want to make 25 stops and take a year to enjoy the journey from one coast to the other or are you wanting and needing to be in NYC in 5 hours? There is no one right way. Be very specific with how and when you want your outcome to manifest, or be open to receive from Spirit that an unexpected path may be the one that will bring your desire in a time frame you may not have considered. If you need or want a quick manifestation of what you desire, be clear about your desired time frame.

Connect to How It Feels Right Now if Your Desire Showed up this Instant

The sixth step is what I call the rapid manifestation step. Without realizing it, we often block our manifestation channels with unconscious fear and doubt. When we create a detailed multi-sensory image of our desire in our mind, it literally becomes real. Be sure to include in your ceremony at least 30 seconds of how you would feel, what you would smell, hear, and taste if your dream were fully present this instant. Go to that place of "my prayers have been answered". The more time you spend on this step the better.

This technique of visualizing with all of your senses, really feeling yourself experience a victory in your mind's eye, is used by world-class athletes and

Olympians. These professionals train not only their bodies but also their minds. They know that our own mind is our biggest enemy in receiving the things we desire and in having success. They spend hours visualizing themselves performing with perfection and they practice the experience of standing on the podium bending to have an Olympic gold medal placed over their head as they hear the National Anthem of their country playing in the background and the crowd bursting with thunderous applause for them. This step erases all doubt and fear. Take in your victory moment fully in your mind's eye. The more time you spend doing this, the stronger your manifestation skills will be. You will be asking yourself, "Why haven't I been doing this all the time?" It only takes a moment and it is amazing. It may also help to practice these steps to manifest small things if your primary desire is something big. Practice makes perfect, as the saying goes.

Offer Gratitude and Celebrate

The final and yet very important step is to offer gratitude to Spirit for the blessing received. Filling your heart with gratitude is a way to shift your mood faster than almost anything I know. Focusing on gratitude for all the good in your life is a helpful tool to use if you feel stuck in any of the previous steps of this process. If you are having a particularly challenging day and you are struggling for what you feel grateful for in that moment, say thank you to Spirit that you have a roof over your head and running water. Give gratitude that you have food to eat and that you can breathe on your own. However basic you need to be, find something to be grateful for and your brain will shift perspective to find more and more things for which you have gratitude that you take for granted every day.

Last but not least, savor the moment and celebrate that you are a powerful manifestor. That you can align with Spirit any time you choose, and that God/Goddess is always there to respond to your request. You are more powerful than you let yourself know. As the inspirational Marianne Williamson reminds us, "Your playing small does not serve the world . . . . As (you) let your light shine, (you) unconsciously give people permission to do the same."

A Husband at Last

The first time I used these steps in an organized way was in November 2003. I turned 40 earlier that year which meant there was no time to waste. Over the years I had created a hodge podge of tools to "call in" or find my husband. I had actually already made two vision boards, and years earlier I had created a list of 20 qualities I desired in my future husband because I had been taught that clarity is important. What I learned in 2003 was how to create a unified field, and it felt so empowering. My manifesting plan was to do a 5-10 minute ceremony daily starting in mid-November, and I set my intention "to meet the man I will marry within one month" from the day I started. I remember distinctly observing myself wince when I put a time frame of one month but I observed this "resistance" which was an inner skeptic saying, "You haven't manifested him in 40 years, how are you going to meet him in the next month"? My new response to myself was, "I am a powerful manifestor, and I now know how to do this! It is time now."

My ceremony involved playing a favorite piece of music, lighting a rose scented candle, stating my intention out loud, and reading a beautiful poem about love and partnership from a card. I focused on the beautiful image of the card and placed a list of characteristics that I wanted my husband to have next to the candle. I had my intention poster for marriage hung on the wall and sometimes danced with it during the ceremony. As I danced to the music I held the image and felt the feelings of what it would be like to dance at my own wedding. I allowed myself to fill with the sensation of unconditional love from a compassionate man who was now my equal partner. I felt the love of the family and friends who would be there to witness our union. I felt the veil on my head and the sway of my long bridal gown. I was amazed at how deep my feelings could go in just a few minutes and how doing this prayer took only 5 minutes yet it left me with a deep sense of peace that stayed with me for the rest of the day.

I started paying attention to things around me in a new way, looking for signs from Spirit. Was it the man who struck up a conversation with me at the gas station? No he didn't seem to be the one. Was anybody inviting me to parties or new events where I might meet new people? How about the neighbor who stopped to chat as he walked his dog? I found myself being more open to conversations with men at church and just about everywhere, but nothing was clicking in a noticeable way. The main thing I noticed was hearing and seeing commercials for E-Harmony™ all the time. I was annoyed! "E-Harmony™, are you kidding me?" I said to Spirit. I heard commercials on the radio and TV, and two people mentioned something about someone they knew meeting a good guy on (what else) E-Harmony™. Luckily I quickly observed this resistance within myself and acknowledge that I needed to follow my intuition if I wanted success with the technique.

As I signed up on-line, one of the first questions was for how many months did I want to join E-harmony™. The options were one month to one year with multiple options in between. I laughed out loud as I chose one month. It took hours to fill out the personality questionnaires about what I liked and disliked. It took me two or three days to complete the process of enrolling. By now it was just 10 days before Thanksgiving and my month was flying by.

I was matched with about a dozen men over that one month period. I excitedly looked at the descriptions and photos of the men I was matched with and started the on-line process of getting to know them within the structure of E-Harmony™. The first couple of matches didn't excite me, but what I noticed in myself was that I wasn't anxious or disappointed by this. I had a calm, inner knowing that as I did my daily 5 minute ceremony the right man was on his way to me somehow. I kept my eyes and ears open to all things, not just E-Harmony™. I became open to idea that the process of meeting men via E-Harmony™ might be a tool to shift my thinking or get me to my goal in some way, or it might be the vehicle through which I met my future husband.

And then the magic happened! On December 9th, 2003, less than 1 month since I started the daily ceremony and set my intention, I was matched with a man whose profile gave me goose bumps. He had many qualities that the other men lacked and we had the same sense of humor. Both of us said that "coffee" was one of the top five things we could not live without. It may sound insignificant, but at the time it was silly things like this that gave me an inner knowing that "this is the one". Most importantly, our spiritual beliefs were in alignment with one another. I remember hitting the button on my computer that would open his photo and saying to myself "I am about to see what my husband is going to look like".

He was dark haired, handsome with loving brown eyes. He had every quality on my list that I placed next to the candle with a few bonus qualities. Most importantly, being with him felt as wonderful and loving and safe as it had felt in my ceremony. I had to get clear about how I wanted it to FEEL to be with my future husband for me to truly recognize that feeling as I was dating.

To my disappointment, we interacted via the E-Harmony™ matching structure and then played phone tag from mid-December into January. We both traveled in January and did not have our first date until February 4, 2004. I remember being in Arizona the last week of January at a work conference finding myself being a little giddy and energized. This type of conference normally would get me a little down because many people brought their spouses and, of course, I did not have one. But again, there was that inner knowing that "divine order is at hand. I am in alignment with Spirit". I met a man at the conference who thought I was fabulous. We were both interested in metaphysical things and he introduced me to some other very interesting people at the conference. I had a ball. He was married and not "the One", but being with him gave me the feeling I had been yearning for: to be with an intelligent, open-minded man who liked to learn new things and who thought I was beautiful and amazing. This experience created the final shift I needed. I remember thinking that my life was about to change as I flew back home to Ohio for my first date with Mark.

I don't always have the clearest memory, but the night of February 4, 2004, is still like a movie in my mind. When I first laid eyes on Mark I felt what I call "soul recognition". What I mean by this is the feeling that you know someone deeply when you are just meeting them for the first time. I have experienced this with only a few people in my life. Sometimes you immediately have a positive response to someone and sometimes it can be negative. This was definitely positive. We had a three hour dinner and talked about everything under the sun. I kept thinking, "I am going to be with this man for the rest of my life," which is NOT a thought I was familiar with. The really wonderful thing was that although I was excited and anxious to meet Mark, I still had that deep inner knowing that what was unfolding was because of my connectedness and Co-creation with Spirit. We had dinner again a few nights later and spoke jokingly of marriage within a month. We were engaged in August of that year and married November 27, 2004, less than a year from our match date on E-Harmony™. We still look at each other lovingly every time we see an E-Harmony™ commercial. One in five people now meet their spouse on an on-line dating site but in 2003 that was not the case. Thank God/Goddess I listened to my intuition about joining E-Harmony™.

The Baby Was On Its Way

My husband Mark and I spoke of our desire for one to two children prior to marrying in November 2004. Because I was 41 and he was 45 when we took our wedding vows, we were ready to receive a child immediately and never used any type of birth control. I remember my nervous excitement each time my period was more than a day late, but the home pregnancy tests always said "Not Pregnant". I focused on hopeful images of famous women like Geena Davis, Anne Liebowitz or Holly Hunter who had healthy children, or even twins, in their mid to late 40's, but deep down I was scared.

After several doctor visits and blood work it became painfully clear that I was in perimenopause at age 42. We saw an infertility specialist, and we were poor candidates for in vitro fertilization unless we used donor eggs. Even though I had worked in an infertility lab in medical school, the idea of donor eggs or surrogacy were completely overwhelming and paralyzing. We talked about adoption but worried we would be told we were too old. I felt really stupid for not freezing my eggs in my 30's or for not getting serious about manifesting a husband sooner in my life.

In May 2008 I attended a four day workshop led by Lisa Michaels using the concepts of her book *Natural Rhythms*™. This a book about how to amplify your manifestation powers by aligning with the elemental forces and getting really clear about your desire. For me it WAS a book about getting pregnant, or should I say, having a baby.

I was lucky to be part of a small group of women who had been students of Lisa Michaels for several years. That May weekend was a four day opportunity for each of us to put what we learned into motion to manifest whatever we desired and to support one another as we each did this. We followed the steps I have outlined for you above. We got clear about our desire and we danced and did ceremony and created artwork and celebrated the fact that our desire was on its way to us in that very moment.

I worked on manifesting a baby with the group of women during the day and my husband and I worked on conceiving the baby each night. I created a ceremony for Mark and me to perform together. We anticipated that we were creating what was to be our child. I slept blissfully each night and completed the last day of the workshop feeling that I had truly integrated the tools that Lisa provided and had an inner peace about the baby's arrival that I had never had before.

A few weeks later when it was clear that I was not pregnant, there was a deep sadness in our home and souls. We felt that God/Goddess had really heard our prayer and answered with a clear "no". There was a myriad of emotions but mostly we felt a deep emptiness and grieved with the knowledge that we would never conceive our own child. I cannot lie, I was angry with God/Goddess and so confused. I had that deep knowing in my core that we were creating our baby that weekend, the same feeling of peace and giddiness I had in the weeks before I met my husband. I asked Spirit for it to be made clear to me what my next role was to be if it was not to be a mother.

Mark and I occasionally discussed adoption but when we explored the process on-line it looked like a long and challenging experience with the vulnerability that we might never be chosen to be a child's adoptive parents. One day in late August, I felt drawn to have an astrology reading by a dear friend Pam Gallagher, who runs an astrology school. Pam knew how important children were to us and advised us that if we were going to take action with adoption we needed to initiate the process in the new moon window for the three days following our reading when there was an astrological energy that would support our desire. She encouraged us to call the adoption agency in that three day window to start the process. As she looked into the coming one to two years there was nothing obvious astrologically that represented a baby coming into our lives, but she did say something new would happen in six months, the first week of February, "and it looks like something big".

We "knew" it couldn't be a baby from an adoption because we "knew" that adopting a newborn was NOT a quick process. She just seemed to be trying to end the reading with something positive to say since a baby one to two years out did not look probable.

I remember feeling anxious and not very hopeful that a baby was possible even by adoption. Pam has been reading my charts each year for 10 years and she's been much too accurate to not see a baby down the pike. The next day I was surprise when I easily found one of the business cards that had been given to me twice in the prior three years by a friend for a local adoption agency run by an adoptive mother. I nervously made the call, spoke to the attorney and owner of the agency and asked for information to be sent to us. The packet was mailed to us quickly but again I was paralyzed by anxiety. Obtaining a home study so that we could be considered by birth parents took about a year to complete with home visits, interviews, medical assessments, letters of recommendation, classes, books to be read, background checks and finger prints. To say it was daunting was an understatement. The packet sat on our kitchen counter from late August until early October.

On October 9, 2008, I received a call out of the blue from an old friend I had not talked to in over six months. Victoria, a single foster mother herself, asked if we might be interested in adopting a baby that was due sometime the next year. I felt like Alice in Wonderland and I had just fallen into another reality where miracles drop out of the sky. Her best friend's niece was unexpectedly pregnant with her second child. My friend knew very little about the birth father except that his relationship with the birth mother was short and precarious and he was only 18. I received the call while in a car full of people that were out of town visitors. I was looking for the right moment to tell my husband this news when he came to me with the phone in his hand the next day saying, "There is a woman on the phone who says we are going to adopt her baby?" My heart leaped into my throat as I took the phone and paced the living room floor in the dark. I spoke to this young woman who very casually was offering us the most sacred of gifts. She said the baby was due at the beginning of February. She invited me to meet her at the hospital the next week to get to know one another and to attend an ultrasound of the baby.

I get dizzy when I think of the rapid sequence of events that unfolded from October 9, 2008, to February 2, 2009. Within two weeks of the initial phone call I was sitting in my car holding ultrasound pictures of "my son".

This was the second ultrasound of the baby and it gave me the needed information to calculate the probable date of conception. Our son was conceived the May weekend of 2008 during the time that my husband and I and my women's group were doing ceremony to create him. From that moment forward I KNEW that this baby was OURS. A powerful lesson on letting go of how we think God/Goddess will answer our prayer.

Mark and I and the staff at the adoption agency went into hyper-drive and completed a home study in record time. It was magical how fast the paperwork was processed and necessary classes showed up at just the right time for us. Our home study was approved one day before we were able to sign the final papers to adopt the baby.

I felt God/Goddess said "NO" to our request for a baby when there WAS a baby on the way to us from that very weekend. We let our egos get caught up in how we thought that our baby should arrive! Thus, step number five: "open to your dream showing up in a surprising way". If I had not listened to my intuition to go see our astrology friend or I had not called the adoption agency when I called, or perhaps, if we had used a different adoption agency, we might still be childless. This brings me back to the premise that God/Goddess only knows how to say yes. Whenever you feel that Spirit is saying no, look for signs that perhaps things are just not showing up in the way or time you envisioned.

I can't wait to hear about your victories and celebrate with you. Please send me your stories and photos at www.NaturalRhythms.org so that you can inspire others to call in their dreams and desires as well. If you have suggestions or tools that worked for you, please share the wisdom; the light is in all of us.

About Tammy Huber-Wilkins MD

Tammy Huber-Wilkins MD is a psychiatrist and Natural Rhythms Creation Coach. Fifteen years in private practice has shown Tammy that some depression and anxiety is caused by the suffocation of our intuition and our divine sacred selves by the frenzy and values of the world around us. Tammy's mission is to assist others to awaken their inner passions and live an authentic life of happiness and fulfillment. Her unique wit and playfulness encourages her clients to have more self compassion and to see their inner beauty and deep wisdom. By using the power of the elemental forces in our everyday life, Tammy knows that anyone can manifest their desires.

Chapter 7

Overcome Your Obstacles & Step Into Your Powerful Self

Judy Keating MA

Obstacle (noun)—something that obstructs or hinders progress.
Overcome (verb) to prevail over (opposition, debility, temptations, etc.);
surmount: *to overcome one's weaknesses.*

I heard the click of the harness as it was closed. I was supported to the
platform, and then asked if I was ready. My heart pounding, I said yes.
The treadmill started to slowly move beneath my feet and my feet would
not move. No matter how much I demanded in my head that they move,
they were unable to step one in front of the other. My feet, stuck in place
on the treadmill belt, traveled behind me and I started to fall. There was
a fast yank on the stop cord and with my legs shaking I was steadied back
on my feet. I was scared and heart-wrenchingly disappointed. I wanted
to be able to walk on the treadmill! It seemed by my most recent attempt
that was not to be. I started to tear up. I wanted to do this so badly. I said
to the therapist helping me,

I said to the therapist helping me, "I really want to be able to do this."

And with resolve, we started again, this time with two people assisting my
efforts to walk.

One of the symptoms of the cerebral palsy, which I was born with, is a
deficit in what is known as proprioception, the sense of the orientation
of one's limbs in space. Experiencing this feeling of disorientation has
sometimes caused me to falsely extrapolate that I did not have reliable

73

input in most areas of my life, especially living in a physical body and being asked to work in a world that relies so much on the tangible.

As I write this, I have just begun a journey to finding my full movement capability. I have been in intense therapy that I had no idea I could utilize. Over a time of nine weeks I have experienced tremendous progress: from barely moving and bent over with most of my weight on a walker to walking harnessed on a treadmill while stepping over objects coming at me on the moving belt and holding myself upright.

Even the therapists had no idea that this was possible. We are all in awe watching my dream of walking independently come more alive with each week that passes. While I do not know the end result, I know in my heart that my unanticipated and catapulting progress is due to the enriched relationship with myself that I gained through my conscious dance with the elements. Elemental wisdom provides me an interactive physical, emotional, mental, and spiritual map that proves invaluable when taking action on my own behalf.

About ten years ago, after much urging from two dear friends, I started working with Lisa Michaels. She introduced me to the elemental wisdom that would shape my life going forward. Each of the elements—Earth, Water, Air, Fire, and Spirit—offered lessons preparing me to do the work necessary to make walking independently a possibility. They also have helped me realize another dream of being qualified to coach others in achieving their own heart-felt desires.

Everyone has elemental gifts. Yes everyone, including you! Each of you reading this has something or more than one something that you do well. It could be cooking, gardening, writing, or being a loving friend. Or it could be the ability and willingness to listen to that inner voice or intuition when it comes in response to the question, "What do I do next?"

Each of your gifts is linked to the elements. When first introduced to the elements, trust that inner voice that says "this is where you will find what you are seeking." One innate, Spirit-given talent is knowing when to follow that inner voice, even if the destination is hidden from view. The elements and their vast teachings can and do meet you precisely where you are, as they did for me.

Human beings each have a unique natural rhythm. This one key teaching of the elements can have a profound impact. Developing a keen and grateful understanding of how each element has a cyclic growth and fallow pattern instills a new respect and honoring of your own natural cycles.

As you begin working with the elemental wisdom, know that it is not uncommon to want something that seems out of reach or beyond your current capability. Your obstacles are no less daunting than the one that was described earlier. This chapter reveals how you can use the elemental forces of Earth, Air, Water, Fire, and Spirit to assist you in finding out where you are unable or unwilling to move forward. With the tools provided in the elemental wisdom and some personal insights for your journey, this chapter assists you in clearing the path to the life your heart desires.

So what are the obstacles in your life? Get comfortable, take a deep breath, and reflect on the obstacles you face. What they are does not matter; what is important right now is that you can view them as a barrier in the way of doing, being, having, or creating the life you desire. Take a moment to write down what you see as your obstacles. Don't edit what you write down, just make a list. When you are finished, put the list down, get up, breathe deeply and stretch. Take a walk, outside if weather conditions permit. Just walk and breathe, walk, and breathe. If walking is not an option, then take some deep breaths and move your body in whatever way you can. Walking, dancing, stretching, and breathing deeply moves the energy, giving your list-making mind a break.

Relaxed, have a look at your list, and pick one obstacle. Whichever one you want!

Now, in relation to that obstacle, answer the following questions using the rating scale below. As you are reviewing these statements, insert whatever your obstacle happens to be into the space marked (_____).

	1 Never True	2 Occasionally True	3 Sometimes True	4 True most of the time	5 Always True
1. The steps it would take to get to the other side of (_____) seem impossible.					
2. I would describe my emotions about (_____) as sad, angry, or overwhelming.					
3. I think that (_____) is bigger than I am.					
4. The things I do to address (_____) are not getting me the results I want.					
5. It seems like I have no choice but to live with (_____).					

Now look at your answers. Which statement or statements have the highest score (meaning that you answered "True Most of the time" or "Always True" in response to that statement)?

Let's look at how to interpret your answer.

If you answered either a 4 or 5 in relation to statement number 1:

You are receiving guidance from the elemental power of EARTH. Earth represents the physical, the foundation, which utilizes structure and form to create the tangible. Having a score of 4 or 5 instructs you that the step-by-step guidance that Earth provides may be of great assistance in overcoming your obstacle. The organic timing of Earth follows a cyclic pattern that no amount of force will successfully alter.

Imagine that you planted seeds in the ground, and they were not sprouting out of the ground two weeks after you planted them. Would you go outside, look at the ground and yell, "GROW!" just because you do not believe that it is happening fast enough? As silly as that image seems, how often do you not respect your own organic timing or natural rhythm? Have you ever wanted to master something and gave up because it seemed to be taking too long? If you have, you are not alone. Would you like to do it differently? You can. Say to yourself, "This is going to take as long as it takes, and just because I don't know how much time is required, that doesn't mean it is not worth it." When you read that statement, how does your body feel: peaceful, startled, sleepy, etc? Observe your body's response to that statement. Your earthly body is a compass to your bliss. Consider detaching from how long something takes, allowing it to unfold, doing what it takes step-by-step, and paying attention to your body's feedback. You will be utilizing the power of Earth to get it done.

So the first thing you can do differently is pay attention to your body's guidance. Yes, even when it tells you things that your mind says are wrong, or when your feelings erupt into judgments, just follow your body's wisdom. Nap, daydream, walk, eat. If you need more Earth to get through an obstacle, your body knows the way. Trust that this is true, because it is. Your body is a magnificent creation designed to bring forth your nature. If it feels different to do this, good! You are following a new path, one that may not be familiar yet. Trust that it will guide you in the ways of surmounting any challenge naturally.

Renowned Life Coach Martha Beck teaches an invaluable tool. She calls it "turtle steps."[1] When you are trying to accomplish anything, particularly those things fraught with obstacles, write out the steps it would take to accomplish the goal. Even if you think the goal is something you believe you can't accomplish, write it out for someone you believe could do it.

Write it out in steps A through Z. Done? Good. Go back to A. Read it aloud.

Step A. Create a web site.

"What? I don't know how to do that! Who am I kidding?"

Sound familiar? If you have that kind of reaction to Step A, one thing is for certain: your step A is much too big. Make Step A into Step a.

Step a. Take a class on creating a web site. "What are you crazy? I don't have the money for that!"

Your body is giving you more information that your step is still too big. Break it down even further, continuing to notice your body's reaction to each new Step a. A small step might be something like looking at two websites and noting what you like and don't like about them. Keep refining your steps until your body responds with, "Oh, I can do that." Then and only then will you have a workable plan worth pursuing. These are turtle steps and they make baby steps appear gargantuan. That's how you'll know them, when your body feels that sense of, "Ah, ok, here I go!" Seems doable right? Way to go! That is the only earthly way to get there, one doable step at a time. Try it. Enjoy your turtle steps. They are laudable because they are moving you toward the thing you want to overcome. As you move forward you may be tempted to up the steps by taking longer strides or setting bigger goals—refrain. Always create a plan that feels easy to you. It will undo years of "can not's" and turn them into "I did it's!"

Nature does not hurry, yet everything is accomplished.
Lao Tzu

If you answered either a 4 or 5 in relation to statement number 2:

Then WATER, the emotional realm, is your teacher in how to change the way you feel about whatever is in your way. This is the key to moving through the obstacle. When you ponder your obstacle and you feel emotionally done in—either by fear, anger, doubt, or defeat—then there is some emotional clearing to be done. Reflect on the obstacle again and ask yourself, "How old was I when I first had these feelings?" Was it 2, 6, 13, 21, your current age? This inquiry is useful as it gives you information about when you may have felt these emotions before, possibly in response to something that was daunting. No matter how old you were when you checked in, what would Love say to, for instance, the 6 year old "you"?

There is no other inquiry that will assist your emotional self more than, "What would Love say or do in this moment?" Whatever the answer, do that for yourself.

Any emotional back talk that comes up (I don't deserve Love, I am not good enough), anything that does not reflect love, is not here to serve your highest purpose. If at first you don't have an answer, it's ok. Just keep asking, "What would Love say or do to care for me?" You will know you have found an answer when you either feel tears, one of the ways that Water helps you move your emotions, or you feel calm, have no thoughts, or you notice that your body relaxes. You may even release a deep breath. These are all guideposts to your emotional body recognizing love.

Another way to assist your emotional self is taking the time to assess whether you feel grief. Any loss, no matter how small or large, can result in the emotion of grief. When grief is left unprocessed or unacknowledged it backs up your emotional flow much like a rock would impede the direct flow of water in a stream. If you are facing a current obstacle is there any loss in your life that could be contributing to the way you are feeling?

For example, have you had a change in your health, job, relationships, and status in your community, home, or any everyday life circumstance? If there has been a change, have you fully mourned any loss around that change? If you feel sadness, grief, depression, or overwhelm, it is possible that you need to fully grieve the loss before you can effectively move forward. In order to recognize and express grief, it is truly helpful to ask for assistance from a trusted relative, friend or a counselor, whatever feels right to you. Seek assistance from someone you trust or feel emotionally safe with while you express your emotions. Asking for help is not always easy and as soon as you do, your load can feel lighter.

There is no right way to express grief. Everyone does it differently. Talking about what you have lost, or writing about it and asking someone you trust to read it, can assist in moving the emotion from a place of static to flowing. Dancing or moving your body to music with the intention of expressing your grief can also be an effective tool for integration and growth.

Your emotions want to evolve with you so that as you grow, your emotional body attains maturity, which gives you the confidence to handle life as it happens, when it happens. Striving for emotional maturity gives you confidence. With confidence, your emotions become a guidance system. Confidence enables you to act without filtering what is right for you through fear. Fear clouds your emotional discernment. Fear is a valid emotion when used to prevent legitimate harm. To live in a constant state of fear prevents anything else from getting through, cutting off your inner water supply. If you operate from a paradigm of fear you become emotionally dehydrated and malnourished. This leaves you bereft of feeling excitement, trust, joy, or true aliveness. A synonym for fear is lack: anytime you focus on what you don't have, you are snuggling up to lack like a bee hooked on bitter honey. "If only I was thinner, taller, smarter, had more (fill in the blank) I'd be happy." Negotiating with "if only" is like bartering with a porcupine for hugs, and wondering why the needles hurt so much!

Here is a favorite emotional growth tool: Love What You Love Full On. Make a list of what you love full on. Here is a sample list:

I love cozy blankets and roaring fires and the sound of the ocean.
I love being able to feel the touch of loved ones and about 3,583 other things.
I love being an awe-struck witness to growth in the human experience and sharing with others.

Make it a mission to live that list on a daily basis and to spend as much time with those people, places, mindsets, information, and activities as possible. What do you love to do? Who do you love to be with? What brings you to that calm, centered present where no obstacle is in your line of sight? What is on your list? Seriously, stop right now and consider these questions and make your own Love What You Love list. Put copies where you see it often: on the fridge, in your desk at work, on the dashboard of your car. Use this list as your emotional appointment calendar. The more you can live your life with this list as your guide, the more your list will grow. You deserve a life filled with love!

You can explore the universe looking for somebody who is more deserving of your love and affection than you are yourself, and you will not find that person anywhere.
Buddha

If you answered either a 4 or 5 in relation to statement number 3:

Then AIR, the mental realm, is an area that is seeking improvement for you. Whatever obstacle you face, what are your thoughts about it? Would it surprise you that sometimes you may not know? Begin by slowing down and seeking to become attentive to what you think. Stopping and taking a few deep breaths is another important tool to becoming more present and calm. When you practice stillness and deep breathing you gain more access to your own inner dialogue. Ask yourself, "What do I want; what do I believe—about myself? About my relationships? About what I am here to do?" Literally, when asking the questions, you might often answer, "I don't know." Many people feel unclear or stuck in this arena. You may have invalid beliefs that you act on as if they are stone cold truth. By becoming mindful or aware of your thoughts, you can begin to change what you think if it is not getting you the results you want. Mindfulness is one of the best gifts you can give yourself.

Do you often say negative or demeaning things to yourself?
"I am not good enough."
"Who do you think you are?"
"I can't be any better, so why try?"

If you recognize yourself in these words, you are not alone. Air provides the tools of focus and intention. Thoughts can run amuck without any discipline. One of the best Air tools comes from best selling author Noah St. John.[2] He practices a system of focusing on positive questions. For example, if you can see that you ask yourself questions in the negative frame such as "Why am I so unhappy?" the mind being the question solving computer that it is, will look for reasons, ways, and data that answers the question why are you "unhappy"? Only answers that fit your question become relevant in your mental awareness, thereby multiplying your unhappiness. Turning your questions in a positive direction, such as "Why am I so healthy?" will set your mind on an evidence-seeking mission to answer that question. While asking yourself positive questions sets your mind in the right direction, you must also take actions that support the new inquiry. Your mind will naturally notice those things that would be healthy like good nutrition, exercise, fresh air, activities that reduce stress. In order to experience the benefits of these activities you must do them. By focusing on positive outcomes you actually change the vibration.

You literally change your mind! Have you ever felt heavy with negative thoughts that you did not know how to change? Lack of awareness of your negative vibration pulls your body down, and creates the lie that your desire is not possible.

As a practice, take a five-minute timeframe where you have no demands and listen to your thoughts. Just receive them, maybe write them down. Reflect on them. Are they positive, energizing, and fruitful? If not, how can you respond to them in a way that refreshes your mental capacity? For example if they are negative, can you imagine having written them on an Etch A Sketch?[3] Remember those fun drawing devices that you could turn over, give them a good shake, and start with a blank slate again? When your thoughts are not enabling, nurturing, or assisting you in going where you want to go, use the Etch A Sketch visual to start anew in your thought process!

Negative thoughts are easy to think, but painful.
Positive thoughts take some effort, but they heal. Make the effort.
Martha Beck

If you answered either a 4 or 5 in relation to statement number 4:

The FIRE element needs some of your attention. Fire serves as the element of action or transformation. With so many things calling for your attention in the modern world, your energy can be drained before you realize it. What fills your tank? If that question feels totally foreign to you, you may suffer from exhaustion and be too tired to ponder an answer. Consider a simple, yet difficult solution: REST! Yes, that's right, rest! Then rest some more. Let yourself rejuvenate, relax, and recoup.

It may seem counter-intuitive, and doing nothing is the most powerful action on the planet. Like one end of a magnet, true rest inspires action. When it is time to flip the magnet, your own Fire knows when to respond. If you will allow yourself to truly sink into that place of peaceful inaction. Think of occasions when you have been involved in experiences that you feel timelessness, that time in space when the world stops and you are intimately involved with whatever you are doing, or whoever you are with. It could be time with a lover, soaking in a tub, spending time in nature, watching a movie, reading a book, or waking up from a lovely nap. Any of these activities put you in a place of "getting out of your own way."

You are getting rest when you begin imagining or daydreaming. Through that lens of relaxation you hear your inner voice say "I'd really like to _____." This is the Fire realm sparking your desire. This spacious place is where tanks are filled. It is a place of light, of passion; of restoring right action.

Your Fire power comes from being willing to take action toward your desires. In a society where often the answer to "What do you do?" defines one's worth, wouldn't it be a different world if you were greeted with, "What lights you up, what do you long to do more than anything?" Why not start giving yourself permission to do just that, act on what you want to do most. Do something—anything—towards getting where you want to be. Make a call, generate an action step lis,t then do number 1, and find information you need to move forward. Any deed done adds momentum which fuels further action.

Finding your own unique pattern of action AND rest aligns you with the energy to make things happen. Discerning those activities, people, and priorities that feed your energy rather than sap it, and using that as a compass to encourage right action assists you in making progress toward your most desired outcome. The acumen of deciding what nourishes your energy takes one thing—practice, practice, and practice. The more you practice, the easier it becomes to utter this one critical word, "No."

Protecting your energy like it is a precious resource is one of the best fire-tending activities you can do. If saying no is unusual for you, start now. While it may be awkward at first, it will get easier. To live fully, you have to say no sometimes. Do you feel obligated to spend time with events, task,s and even people that do not light you up? Understand that obligation is not a vital reason to do anything. Of course there are things you must do, even if you don't like them. To enliven your inner Fire and have the fuel to be proactive in accomplishing what you truly want, you have to determine through your own will what you will let go out of your life.

When you do what you need to do to restore your energy, taking action steps towards transforming your obstacle becomes doable. The most important thing is to do something! Alter the circumstances that cause you suffering. Get whatever support you need to keep taking action steps. As hard as the first steps seem, once you get going, the momentum and the re-igniting of your passion for what you really desire will serve to keep fueling the next steps. Kindle your own light then share your radiant self with the world. Your brightness can illuminate the darkness of whatever obstacle you are working with to overcome and allow you to see where to take your next step.

As far as we can discern, the sole purpose of human existence
is to kindle a light in the darkness of mere being.
Carl Jung

If you answered either a 4 or 5 in relation to statement number 5:

Then you may need to open more to working with SPIRIT. As defined by Lisa Michaels, Spirit is your connection to the divine. It is the spark of Spirit that is you. It is your connection to God/Goddess.[4] Spirit is in all the elements and in all that humans can know. Spirit infuses everything with a grace-filled cohesiveness. Spirit can move both in the outer world assisting in the manifestation of your creations and in your inner landscape helping to interpret your outer experience.

Ask whatever obstacles you are working with: How has it taught you valuable lessons? How has it improved your ability to cope? What lessons has it given you that nothing else could have? The answers to these questions are ones that you co-create with Spirit. The elemental power of Spirit is the power of choice. If you are having difficulty seeing any good when considering your obstacle, can you make a different choice? If you are willing, even briefly, to acknowledge that your life has a higher purpose and meaning which has value beyond what you can conceive, this invites Spirit to move in your life. Spirit can work in ways you don't always understand. Choosing to see the good in any circumstance changes your stance from one of opposition to one of acceptance. Only when you are willing to accept life as it is without fighting it, are you able to choose something different.

You are one of a kind and your being here matters, maybe more than you ever thought before now. It may be difficult for you to believe that statement; nonetheless, it is true! Spirit moves through you and in you;

this is the experience of your own unique essence. If you choose to belittle or deny what "wants" to be articulated by your life, it is lost not only to you, it is lost to anyone or anything that could have been uplifted by your willingness to share your gifts or those experiences, viewpoints, feelings, and events that are only yours to give.

You are unrepeatable. There is a magic about you
that is all your own.
D.M. Dellinger

Believe it or not, when I first agreed the assignment to write this chapter, my balance was in such a precarious place that I had been using a wheelchair intermittently and had decided I needed to buy one instead of rent one. I had been fighting very strongly where I was with my balance for a few years, determined to overcome the way things were at that time. The only way I knew to survive what was happening was to "hold on tight" to the mobility I currently had, which was unpredictable. When I could see the wheelchair as something that really made things easier, and I could have compassion for my body that was so tired of fighting to walk, things began to shift. I finally surrendered control of whether I walked or not, gave up fighting what I thought was the worst thing that could happen (my having to use a wheelchair), and things began to change. This is an example of the power of Spirit and releasing attachment to how something will manifest. I held on so tightly to things not changing. The only outcome from my limited line of sight was that things would get worse if I released the reigns of being the one in charge of whether I walked or not.

The incident that began this chapter had me struggling with the treadmill just after my surrender to the wheelchair. I am blessed to have found a new physician who directed me to a rehabilitation facility that could offer someone with my diagnosis a treatment plan.

What I know now is that I needed the foundation and skills learned from Lisa's *Natural Rhythms* teachings in preparation to fully utilize my elemental capabilities on the path to independent mobility. More clarity came during a workshop with some friends when the phrase, "I am basking in uncertainty, knowing all will be okay," passed through my mind. It is the true opposite of "floundering in doubt" which had been my usual stance. I realized it is the phenomenal understanding that basking in uncertainty is where co-creation with Spirit needs to "groove" in order to accept the unpredictability of my condition and to be in true co-creation with Spirit. While I might have eventually worked with the same therapists, the results probably would not have been as extraordinary!

Notice that obstacles are a part of life and when an obstacle has been surpassed, there very well might be others to negotiate. The shared experience of obstacles, creates a common bond that all can understand. Each of the elements, EARTH, WATER, AIR, FIRE, and SPIRIT, teaches through their natural expression in the world. By experiencing the elements in relation to you, one can learn from them and apply their wisdom to your life.

This chapter concludes with a set of questions that gives you information about how far you have come and where you might need to continue working with overcoming obstacles. The statements are listed one to five. Just like the initial inquiry, each statement applies to an element in the order of Earth, Water, Air, Fire, and Spirit. Before taking the quiz, think again of the obstacle you have been working on. In this questionnaire you will read the statement, inserting whatever your obstacle is or was in space marked (_____) and then score yourself 1-5.

Post-Chapter Check In	1 Never True	2 Occasionally True	3 Sometimes True	4 True most of the time	5 Always True
1. When working with (____), I have a great foundation and feel able to take the next step.					
2. When I consider (_____), I feel self-love and acceptance.					
3. When I think about (_____), my thoughts support me now and in the future.					
4. In regards to (_____), I am able to let go of what is not moving me forward in life.					
5. I have compassion for myself and am willing to ask for support to co-create my life around (_____).					

Any and all answers of 1-2 in this set indicate that you could benefit by working more with that particular element. Remember, the elements meet you where you are, and the journey with the elements is a life-long endeavor. There is no right or wrong in your answers, just a reading of where you are in this moment.

For more information on other ways you could apply the elemental teachings in your life, continue reading to get advice from the other experts. I wish you success on your journey and fun along the way!

About Judy Keating, MA

Judy uses her over 17 years experience in Human Resources as well as her keen intuition and a lifetime of experience in surmounting challenges to inspire both individuals and groups to find new ways to interact with life. Judy possesses a calm presence, unique sense of humor, and wise understanding of how we contribute to our own suffering. Judy assists her clients to rekindle their joy, life force and ease by reacquainting them with the elemental forces of nature through experiences, tools, play, and introspection. She is a certified Creation Coach through the Natural Rhythms Institute and is trained in both life and nature-based coaching. To download Judy's free coaching tool "*7 ways to diminish overwhelm*" go to www.innerlifecoaching.net.

Chapter 8

Quality Life Mastery:
Eight Steps for Rhythmically Harnessing Success

Chantal Debrosse

Mother Nature has been my best teacher. I've known her since I was a child. From dancing in the rain to lying down on the grass imagining what animals the clouds would morph into, I was happy when I was in Nature. Each contact with Nature gave me the relaxing feeling I needed since life at home was a bit dysfunctional. When I spent time in Nature, I had nothing but good experiences. Soon I grew up and put these "childish" things aside. I became an overachieving teenager and was motivated by having good grades. I jumped into life feet first and juggled all my goals at once. I was able to complete my Bachelor's degree while being married, working full time, and raising one child with another one on the way. Life was tough, but I was tougher. I would push through every obstacle that came my way because that is how I was able to make things happen for me.

This sounds like a story of achievement, but the story is actually one of "over" achievement. That is, I was flying over the place where achievement lives but never landing there. I was always up in the air attempting to balance more than I could fit on my plate. Only when I decided to stop trying so hard did I find myself on solid ground. Once I stopped pushing and started allowing, I found more peace and even more accomplishments. While I've been actively involved in what I call "the machinery" of the corporate world for over 25 years, I found my way back to Nature. Not only do I look at her beauty, I now embrace her cycles and have grasped their deeper meanings.

This shift came about over time. But there is one day that stands out in my memory where Nature pulled me out of the dumps. I was at work and was walking from one building to another. I was alone with my depressing thoughts contemplating the pain of my own codependence and my unhappy marriage. All at once, my usual sadness was halted abruptly when I noticed some of the goings on in Nature. As I approached my destination, I noticed wasps busily buzzing around a bush. I saw ants doing their work and I noticed that I sensed no sadness or anxiety in them. Yes, they have their challenges like being eaten alive or poisoned by pesticides. Yet it struck me that they don't worry about that. They just go on. I then thought about what else in Nature goes on—birds fly, fish swim, trees grow, flowers bloom. I went further in my musing and thought about how there is a cadence to life and that the seasons are a continuous cycle of natural events. I saw that life has a beat and that beat persists, the rhythm continues, the cycles carry on.

Nature helped me to move forward and began to search for how I could be more present in my life instead of allowing myself to replay old tapes of what happened to me and why I was so miserable. I began to search for deeper meaning. There is a human merry-go-round, "the machinery", where we repeat the same things over and over and over again while convincing ourselves that this is the purpose of our lives: new cars, bigger homes, more popularity, and so on. But there is a natural merry-go-round that is truly merry. It is the Wheel of the Year. Instead of creating a repetitive rut, Nature shows us that we can work with the cycles and succeed in our activities the way an experienced surfer succeeds in riding a wave.

My first encounter with Nature teachings was during a class on the Native American Medicine Wheel. Nearly a decade later, I was participating in my first *Natural Rhythms*™ program with Lisa Michaels as our facilitator. This program has been designed to guide each of us in deepening our spiritual connection with the Divine as we rediscovered our relationship with Nature's elemental forces. It was then that I learned how the elemental forces are expressed in our daily lives.

In that very first gathering, I was impressed with how Nature's rhythmic cycle is not something that happens around me, but something that happens within me and within everything around me. From that point on, I began my journey to consciously create my life by observing the rhythm of Nature and the rhythm in me so that I could access deeper levels of my inner wisdom.

I started to actively work with the Wheel of the Year in 2005. I have learned to follow these steps when I am working on any project or going through any life experience. While it's not necessary to wait until the phases match what is happening on the calendar in order for you to use them, if you find you are in sync with the calendar, use the timing to your advantage so that Nature itself will join you in your endeavors. Following these steps, you will have developed a deeper understanding of how to handle any project from the beginning to its end and into a new beginning.

By the end of this chapter you will have written in a journal, made a vision board, and created some very powerful affirmations for yourself. I mention smudging and vision board and they may be terms or concepts that are unfamiliar to you. Therefore, I have included an explanation for each one so that anyone reading this material will be capable of easily following the steps that I have outlined.

Step 1—Samhain and the Halloween Phase

Do you remember wearing costumes, bobbing for apples, and eating candy till you couldn't eat another bite? Well, now you can add another reason to love Halloween. The Celts call it Samhain (SOW-win) which means "end of summer" when days are getting shorter and nights are getting longer. This phase corresponds to the lunar cycle of the Balsamic Moon, which is the last sliver of moon before it can no longer be seen in the sky. This is the phase when the seed is buried underground. During this time of transition, what once existed no longer exists in the same form. You are in the Air realm as you are contemplating the beginning of a whole new cycle.

- Wheel—Samhaim, Halloween
- Element—Air (thoughts, communication)

Physical Connection
You can decorate with autumn leaves and flowers, gourds, squashes, corn. Get into the spirit of the season.

Mental Intention

Focus your intention on keeping negative things from your past out of your future. Use the power of your imagination to redirect and release any past hurts that may want to come during this time when your new ideas are vulnerable to being chased away by old ways of thinking. The new idea seed is newly planted and you must be vigilant in making sure you filter out what of your past is holding you back. These negative ideas can be transmuted into their positive equivalent. Thus greed turns into generosity, corruption turns into integrity, and betrayal turns into fidelity. Allow yourself to be open to receive knowledge from your ancestors or historical persons you admire. Imagine what advice they would give you and write it down.

Mental Exercise

I use my understanding of this phase of the Wheel of the Year to tap into the gifts it has to offer. I do not wait until Halloween to access this energy. Any time I am about to embark on a new way of thinking or a new aspect of business, I call in the energy[1] of Samhain. Any time I am at a new beginning and have no clue as to how I am going to start, I call in the energy of Samhain. Pondering Samhain allows me to remember that my new ideas are buried within and need to be patiently nurtured in order for them to yield the intended harvest later on. I recommend spending a few moments in Nature and lighting a candle when you come back inside. Take a few moments to contemplate this statement:

To be born to the new we must die to the old.
Journal whatever comes up for you. What does this mean to you? Can there be a new meaning coming up for you? Let your wise voice speak and take time to honor it by listening to it.

Step 2—Yule and the Winter Solstice Phase

When you are starting a business, you are in the dark while formulating your ideas which are permeated with possibilities, just like healthy soil. You use Earth practices such as setting a plan and deciding the structure of your business.

When I was a little girl, I could not stand Winter Solstice because it was the longest night of the year. I would fret about the loss of summer and being in the middle of the school year. It wasn't until I started working with the cycles in the Wheel that it struck me that while the Winter Solstice was the shortest day of the year, it was the last day of darkness and the sun would take hold of the sky an average of one extra minute per day. Since then, it has become a favorite point in the cycle of life.

Winter Solstice corresponds to the New Moon where the moon can no longer be seen in the sky. The New Moon is the phase where the seed is in the ground. The death of the seed holds the promise of the new plant. In the dark silence is found an opening to life.

- Wheel—Winter Solstice
- Element—Earth

Physical Connection
You can decorate with the usual winter greenery such as evergreens and wreaths to represent rebirth and the circle of life. Have candles and holiday lights in your home. Place lots of sparkly ornaments and prisms and tinsel wherever you like in order to create as much light as possible. Place a large bowl of water and a candle in the center of the room. Offer a free gift to your customers.

Mental Intention
This is a natural time for letting go and saying farewell. Release your resentments and regrets into the darkness, knowing they will be transformed. Write about them in your journal or write them on slips of paper which you can burn in your transformational Yule fire. Use your holiday cards to make amends to people you've hurt or neglected. Keep in mind that this is the time for you to welcome the light as it makes its return in your daily life.

Mental Exercise
I recommend finding a moment to spend in Nature. When you come back inside, light a candle. Without having to recall any old hurts, take a deep breath and exhale, releasing all tension and all old, limiting, stagnant thoughts. Give yourself a break by taking a few moments to contemplate this statement:

In the darkness I hear the whisperings of my new beginning.
Journal whatever comes up for you. What does this statement mean to you? Can there be a new meaning coming up for you? Remember to let your wise voice speak and take time to honor it by listening to it.

Step 3—Imbolc and the Groundhog Day Phase

You choose seeds that you begin to plant. Earth activities must continue to ensure all is in its proper place.

As a kid, I thought the groundhog was an animal that had some old special powers that somehow allowed him to predict how much more winter weather there would be. Growing up in sunny South Florida, I saw it as a cute tradition. Little did I know that Groundhog day was formerly called Candlemas and Imbolc. No matter what its name, it is the halfway point between Winter Solstice and Spring Equinox. No matter what the groundhog said, there was six more weeks left in the official winter season. Again, I found myself becoming enamored with another point in the cycle of life. Imbolc corresponds to the Waxing Crescent Moon where the moon is just barely able to be seen. The Waxing Crescent Moon is the phase where the seed in the ground. The opening of the seed holds the promise of the new plant.

On Imbolc, the Wheel of the Year turns us back to spring. This is the day when the Sun's rays begin to grow in strength. Longer days approach and in some places the first signs of spring emerge. Imbolc is a Celtic term for spring which means "in the belly" (i mbolg). It is a time for allowing yourself to be fertile with inspired ideas. To ensure success, it is important to harness the divine energy which ensures a steady supply of business so that six months from now you can begin to reap the fruits of your efforts.

- Wheel—Imbolc
- Element—Earth

Physical Connection
Now is a good time to declutter. Go through closets, attics, and basements, and give away clothes and toys that have been outgrown. Cleanse the house from top to bottom. This is a great time to be charitable. Once

you've decluttered, set a designated space for you that is sacred and will be maintained well. Add white and yellow flowers and candles.

Mental Intention
Turn on every single light in your home or office, from the bright kitchen lights to the closet lights to the smallest nightlights. Focus your energy on luring back the sun and wooing your riches. Think to yourself that as there is more light, there is more growth.

Mental Exercise
I recommend finding a moment to spend in Nature. When you come back inside, light a candle. Give yourself a break by taking a few moments to contemplate this to statement:

Beneath the snow, the seedling is breaking through the ground.
Journal whatever comes up for you. Are you looking forward to all the potential that will begin to blossom in the spring? Can there be another way to look at this statement? Listen to your wise voice as it speaks to you. Taking the time to honor it is taking the time to honor you.

Step 4—Ostara and the Spring Equinox Phase

I don't know why this was such an exciting time for me, but I was fascinated by the balance of equal light and dark. From this point the light continues to grow. This time corresponds to the Lunar cycle of the First Quarter Moon, which looks like a half moon. You have reached the point where you know half of what you need to know.

But instead of staying in the seedling stage, use the element of Fire to cause the seeds to sprout. Only when they sprout can you ever hope of seeing a future harvest. That is why the fiery action is needed. The threats from frost are virtually over.

- Wheel—Spring Equinox
- Element—Fire

Physical Connection
Fill your place with local flowers. Maybe the willows are changing their color as the sap tentatively rises, making for a good altar decoration. Watch the dawn, and do some visualization. Light incense and smudge[2] your home. Plant the seed of a perennial or an annual focusing your intent strongly on the seed, then on the pot of soil after you have planted it. Take care of it. The plant can continue to flourish with your care. Keep honoring and connecting with Nature. Have a special place for this. Celebrate with positive people.

Mental Intentions
Write down your plan for what you want to accomplish in the coming months. Allow yourself to call forth all the new things you want to bring into your life and write them down. Create a vision board[3] that has pictures of things that represent your desire and keep it in a place where you can see it at least twice a day.

I recommend finding a moment to spend in Nature. Notice the changes that have taken place in your surroundings, such as the return of more color and the amount of growth that has come forth. When you come back inside, light a candle.

Mental Exercise
Meditate on those things you want to grow during the year including patience, compassion, wisdom, understanding, etc. In the fertile ground of your mind, imagine each idea is a seed that you have planted. Allow yourself to water these seeds and see them blossoming and coming to life. When you come back inside, light a candle. Give yourself a break by taking a few moments to contemplate this statement:

I am blooming and blossoming in the time of spring.
Journal whatever comes up for you. Are you looking forward to all the potential that will begin to blossom in the spring? Can there be another way to look at this statement? Listen to your wise voice as it speaks to you. Taking the time to honor it is taking the time to honor you.

Step 5—Beltane and the May Day Phase

Beltane is also known as the first of May celebration. This time in the annual cycle celebrates the visible arrival of spring, warmth, and the light. This time corresponds to the Lunar cycle of the Gibbous Moon, which is which looks like an almost full moon. The emphasis is on the victory of the light over the night. This is a good time to be very active in your pursuits if you want to have tangible success. A tradition for Beltane celebrations is jumping over bonfires. Imagine a challenge that you are facing and make yourself jump over it. Do this with each little obstacle that comes your way. Live in complete gratitude for Nature's generosity. Celebrate your progress on the Wheel. Celebrate how far you have come.

- Wheel—May Day, Beltane
- Element—Fire

Physical Connection
Colors are the Rainbow spectrum. Beltane is a festival of flowers, fertility, sensuality, and delight. It is the best time to go out camping and admire the new spring flowers.

Mental Intention
The focus of your intention is to remain steadfast at this point. As your attention increases, do not allow it to waiver. It is tempting to jump into all the opportunities that will seem to be available to you at this time. Take care to balance your joy and burgeoning success with discernment. Focus on what or who you wish to nurture and what or who nurtures you in return in a manner that allows you to be healthy, profitable, and keeps you moving toward your intended outcome.

Mental Exercise
Sit in a comfortable and quiet place with your journal and pen. Meditate on the accomplishments you've made since the Samhain part of the thought process. Give yourself a minute to write each one down as quickly as possible. Look at the list and close your eyes. Imagine that you are standing on fertile ground. In the fertile ground, imagine each accomplishment is a blossoming flower. Each blossoming flower multiplies itself and you have a field of blooming flowers. If you are prone to allergies, pretend these flowers are harmless and actually have healing properties just for you. Now pick a

flower. The petals fall away to show the center is a gold coin. Pick as many as you like. Fill your pockets with them. On your way back home, give to a person in need. Feel the joy of receiving and giving. Give yourself a break by taking a few moments to contemplate this statement:

I am surrounded by Nature's abundance. I am abundant.

Journal whatever comes up for you.

Step 6—Mid-Summer and the Summer Solstice Phase

As the name "Midsummer" indicates, this is considered the height of the summer. Yet there is an undertone of darkness in the light. The Summer Solstice is the time when the sun is in its glory. This is the longest day of the year and the shortest night. While we celebrate the power of the sun, we also note its decline. From now on, the hours of sunlight will decrease. It is the longest day, having the most sunshine in a 24 hour period. Now is the time to call in the element of Water as you set up a system for your business to practically run itself. This time corresponds to the Lunar cycle of the Full Moon.

- Wheel—Summer Solstice
- Element—Water

Physical Connection

Go camping or go to the park. This is a time for interaction with Nature and to meet new people. Fashion flowers into wreaths and wear them. Use symbols that represent light and warmth to you: golden discs, sunflowers, shiny metal trays, chili pepper lights. Honor Water by filling a bowl with water, adding some floating candles and some flower heads. Take a flower to the nearest moving body of water, make a wish, kiss the flower, and throw it into the water to carry your blossomed wish to its intended destination.

Mental Intention

The focus of your intention is to stand fully in the light. You are required to show up and be counted. Networking in your field is crucial. Your marketing efforts must be stepped up. You may need to revise and renew your resume even if you are not job hunting. If you are not self-employed, it's time to present that idea at work. Do not waiver at this point. Keep an eye on your intended outcome.

Mental Exercise

Sit in a comfortable and quiet place with your journal and pen. Meditate on moving into the full light. Imagine that you are surrounded by a white gentle light. You are alone. You are at peace. Look around you and you see you are floating in an orb of light. The orb that you are in floats gently down to a garden. In that garden you find there are people moving about with their ideas in their hands. Each one is engaged with the others speaking about their invention and sharing what they have done. Some inventions are new processes or new intellectual property while others are more tangible like cars or appliances. Off in the corner to your left you see a dark spot. A few people seem to be standing there frozen. You ask someone what is going on there, and they say that these are the people who are afraid to share their ideas. You ask how can they join the happiness that everyone else is feeling. The answer is that they must believe that they can and that is how they join in. Tell them you have an idea and share your idea. Feel your heart opening and fill it with compassion for those who are afraid to show up. On your way back home give. Feel the joy of receiving and giving on yet another level. Take a few moments to contemplate this statement:

There is more light. The fire grows. Action is taking a life of its own.

Journal whatever comes up for you.

Step 7—Lammas and the First Harvest Phase

Lammas is the beginning of the harvest cycle. As the first harvest, it is an excellent time to share with others. The moon is beginning to wane away. A bountiful harvest insures that we have the tools and supplies we need to enter into the next inward phase. You are still in the system development phase; however, you are moving toward less light, moving inward to add more products to your business offerings. Levity, joy, and festivity are as much a part of the process as endings and new beginnings. Harvesting what we have planted makes the efforts worth doing and allows us to connect with our ability to create. Each experience opens a window into ourselves, into who we were, who we are, and who we are choosing to become This time corresponds to the Lunar cycle of the Disseminating Moon.

- Wheel—Loaf Mass, Lammas
- Element—Water

Physical Connection
If you didn't get around to doing your spring cleaning, do it now. Donate any old clothes, toys, school supplies, etc. that you no longer need. Decorate your home with sunflowers, lilies, seashells, summer fruits and flowers, feather/flower door wreaths, sun dials. Use the colors red, orange, golden yellow, green, light brown, gold, bronze. Celebrate with loaves of homemade bread, berries, apples, seasonal fruits and vegetables.

Mental Intention
Lammas is a time of personal reflection on the harvest of our thoughts, actions, deeds, events, and experiences. The harvest can be the wealth of experiences we have attained regardless of whether they were gains or losses. We are richer and stronger as a result of those experiences.

Mental Exercise
Sit in a comfortable and quiet place with your journal and pen. Meditate on perseverance. Think of a person that you admire whose life story entails triumph over trials, losses, and obstacles. If you know his/her life story, think about how much perseverance s/he had. If you don't remember the details, check out a book about him/her at the library or research online. Focus on the ability to overcome. Think about your abilities to overcome, how you have overcome, and how you have grown. Take a few moments to contemplate this statement:

We develop by experience, not by chance.
Connect to the theme of perseverance and change. Take stock of what has worked and what you may need to give up to ensure further success. Are there any stumbling blocks and doubts that may be plaguing your thoughts? Which habits or attitudes have gotten in your way and which ones have opened doors for you? Journal whatever comes up for you.

Step 8—Mabon and the Autumnal Equinox Phase

I have to admit that, growing up, this was not one of my favorite times of the year. School had just started and summer was definitely over. Again, as I gained a more mature outlook on this time of the year, I realized once more that it was yet another gift from Mother Nature. During the Autumnal Equinox, we reach the point of equal light and dark, and we are moving back into an inward phase. You are making a full circle back to the element of Air as you deepen your understanding of your business and your place in the world. This is the second harvest. There is still time to reap from your activities. The one product you had may have been leveraged into two or more products. This time corresponds to the Lunar cycle of the Last Quarter Moon, which is which looks like a half moon.

- Wheel—Mabon, Autumnal Equinox
- Element—Air

Physical Connection
Decorate with seasonal elements such as gourds, stalks of wheat, corn, or any items that connect you with the season. Smudge by burning in a fire-safe container any incense or dried herbs from your garden such as rosemary or sage.

Mental Intention
This is a time when the harvested plants are setting their seeds. They are preparing themselves for their new cycle. Taking a clue from Nature, this is not the end of everything, but the conclusion of a cycle that is preparing itself for a new beginning. Think of the goals you've accomplished over the summer and the people who were there to assist and support you. Show yourself appreciation for your efforts and tell each person how much you have appreciated their help.

Mental Exercise
Imagine you are seeing the sun move across the sky in three seconds and it disappears for three seconds. Repeat this a few times until you are in touch with this rhythm of equal light and dark. When you feel connected and balanced within, ask yourself where do you need more balance in your life. Do you need more sleep? More satisfaction in your work? More time for creativity? More time in Nature? Allow yourself to explore how

you can have more personal balance in your life. Take a few moments to contemplate this statement:

Abundance begins with gratitude.
Journal whatever comes up for you.

Benefits from Mother Nature

Being aware of the inward and outward movement of the tides of life can help you in your personal and spiritual growth. This awareness allows you to reconnect with Nature's cycles so that you will understand the starting and ending of the seeds of a project you have been working on, or the seeds of your career, family relations, personal creativity, or education.

Rediscovering Mother Nature as my ally has greatly reduced my anxiety level as I found a way to see the steps that must be taken at specific times to yield the greatest levels of success. With this eight step process that has been created for us by Nature herself, I find that my ideas no longer remain hidden, songs no longer remain unsung, and dances no longer remain un-danced. I have become kinder to myself by giving to myself the same compassion I give others. While it may seem paradoxical, I have actually achieved more by being at peace. Any time I do experience stress it is when I forget that everything is alright, I find that those moments happen less often and last for a day or a minute instead of a year or a decade. Keeping in mind the cycles and phases of Nature has given me the life mastery I had been searching for throughout my life.

With Nature's guidance, I have learned how to stay open and aware of the infinite possibilities that surround me. I have also learned how I can participate in the co-creation of my world. But the best lesson I have learned from Nature is that I am a part of a balanced system where everything and everyone in it matters. I am always supported.

Notes

What is calling in energy?

Any time you read "calling in energy", this means taking the time to think about a particular thing. Through our thoughts we have access to what anything has to offer. For example, if you have a very intelligent dog that learns new tricks easily, you may see that as an example of being mentally flexible. In this case you would like to tap into the energy of mental flexibility. Visualize the dog and feel what being able to learn easily feels like. I recommend practicing this with any attribute you would like to obtain. This is not taking away any energy from anyone or anything, but rather tapping into the fountain that is there for everyone.

2. What is smudging?

Smudging is a simple ceremony for spiritual cleansing that is intended to assist you into moving your mind deeper into the spiritual connection you will be having with each mental exercise I have listed. To smudge, you will have incense or herbs burning in a fire-safe container. Blow out the flames so that you only have the smoke. Gently wave the smoke from the burning herbs over your body as you take slow, deep breaths. After smudging, continue to breathe deeply and enjoy the scents until you are in a relaxed state of mind.

If you are allergic to smoke, you can either spray yourself with a gentle scented oil or scented water or make a paper fan and use the power of your mind as you imagine clearing your energy of any negativity by fanning them away.

3. What is a vision board?

A vision board, also called a vision map, is a visual tool that helps you to maintain your focus on a life goal by allowing you to clarify what you want and concentrate on it. You can use any surface such as a poster board, a piece of cardboard, a piece of wood or even cloth where you will glue, stitch, or staple images that represent what you desire in your life. The value of the vision board is that it helps to keep you from being distracted from and forgetting about your dreams. Briefly, a vision board helps you as you dream it, believe it, and take steps to achieve it!

About Chantal Debrosse

A modern day philosopher and visionary with over 25 years of experience in the corporate world, Chantal uses her intuitive skills and expansive spiritual experience to lead her employees and to coach others into their own greatness. Chantal holds a Bachelors degree in Professional Management, is a CTA Certified Life Coach, and a Natural Rhythms Institute trained facilitator. Chantal uses all of these philosophies at her disposal and blends them into a unique and comprehensive perspective of what it takes to master the human experience while working in conjunction with the natural timing of Mother Nature.

Chapter 9

Connect to the Soul of Your Home to Bring Happiness and Harmony to Your Hearth

Paula York

True imagination is not fanciful daydreaming; it is fire from heaven.
Ernest Holmes

At the age of six years old, I had my first *House Whisperer* experience. I was too young to understand how this event would call forth future synchronicities that would shape my life as an intuitive designer of the home and soul. In that moment, I knew something really big had happened and for a long time I kept it a secret. Somehow, I thought talking about it would take away its mystery. Later, I realized I was given a glimpse into a window that had revealed the pathway to my life's purpose.

I loved playing in daydreams of order and beauty. In my mind's eye I could see the clothes I would fashion for my dolls and later for myself. The room behind my eye became a way to entertain myself. Every morning when I got on the school bus I would settle in, close my eyes and begin to *feel* my way to school. I would peek now and then to see if we were where I thought it felt like. I soon discovered I knew who was getting on the bus by *feeling* who they were before I looked to see if I was right. I can still remember the first time I knew there was a letter from my Australian pen pal waiting for me in the mailbox. I got off the bus, ran to the mailbox with an inner knowing that it would be there. After the second or third time this happened, I decided to see if I could guess what she would talk about in her next letter. We sent letters back and forth always knowing what the other would be talking about. Some 45 years later, we still have this inner knowing of what is going on with each other. As a child, I thought what I heard, felt, and saw was something that everyone did.

A few months before my maternal grandmother passed away, she tried to tell me that I had the ability to *feel* what other people *feel,* but she didn't know what to call it. I can still feel her hand touching my arm as she made me promise her that I would not stop *listening* and *feeling.* These are but a few of the many synchronicities that followed as I continued to window-shop my way to understanding my life's purpose as an intuitive empath. I not only experience emotions of other people, but the feelings and energy of the space where they live or work. I tap into unseen worlds that make and shape our physical environments.

My First House Whispering Experience

Understand that you will be like those with whom you SURROUND yourself. Your environment is stronger than YOU are.
Author unknown

I ran to the house from the dairy barn where my paternal grandfather and uncle were dueling with a cane and a tobacco stick. I did not want to see what they would do to each other, so I ran. My grandfather, who was blind, had placed one hand on the hindquarter of a cow and he knew immediately that it was the wrong cow for that stall. When I got inside the house I shut my eyes tight and began to twirl round and round. I extended my arms and hands to touch whatever was there. For the first time, I felt the difference in the dining room chairs and understood how he knew if I had moved them even though he could not see them. To me, my sister and cousins they all looked the same, but that day the world of vibration opened up for me. Every chair felt different than the next.

Like my uncle, our attempts to fool him with moving things around never worked. It didn't matter if it was a cow, the dining room chairs, or one of us, he always knew with a simple touch of the hand what had been moved or who entered the room. Even more perplexing was how he could identify which grandchild he was hearing walk across the floor. We would try to trip him up by shuffling around and extending our arms for him to feel.

As always, he knew whose arm he was touching without us saying a word. I would go home, thinking to myself, "How, does he do that?"

Later, I came to understand that my blind grandfather gifted me with the ability to see beyond my physical eyes. I began deeply listening to the vibrations in a room, just like he did. My young mind took in every interaction I had with my grandfather in such a way that I integrated some of the abilities of the blind. Some might call it a sixth sense. For me, it was natural to use the eyes behind my eyes.

At twelve, I had my first experience of hearing those on the other side. My paternal great-grandfather came to give me a message after we moved into his house. I was not happy to be sleeping in the same room where he had died. When I saw him, I first thought I was dreaming. Not until I pulled my hair and pinched myself while hiding under the bed sheet did I realize he was truly standing next to my bed. My next peek from under the sheet gave me a deep sense of peace as he gave me a message I could hear and feel in my being. I knew I would be safe and that he was watching over me. I know without a doubt that both my grandfather and great-grandfather along with others that have passed send me *house whispers* from the unseen world.

I've always had an intensity in setting up my home or any space for that matter. I know when furniture is functionally or energetically in the wrong place. It is also easy for me to discern what a restaurant or office needs to shift the energetic and visual ambiance. When I purchased my *Decorating Den*[1] franchise I was in heaven. It gave me a way to bring the *whispers* into a space without really talking about it to my client unless they seemed open to suggestions other than color and style. I have said more prayers over houses than I can count. When the Feng Shui wave hit the states I read and read and read every book I could get my hands on. It was natural for me and made sense in the whole scheme of what works and what does not work in a home. I became a certified Feng Shui consultant in the mid 90's. This was an amazing journey in itself and I was fortunate to study with a Chinese Master.

When I discovered *Natural Rhythms*, my understanding of the elements was already solid. I had no idea how integrating the elements would amplify my abilities. The elements have joined in on sending *whispers* that help guide me into what a space needs to dance in harmony and balance. I also worked with a major retailer for six years as one of 34 national window and furniture manager/trainers, where I continued to deepen my understanding of what an American consumer desires in their home. I bring a unique mix of in-home and retail experience that is enriched with *house whispers* from the unseen world. I see, I listen and then translate the meaning within the *whispers* as it relates to a given space or person.

As our inner elemental teachers guide us toward growth, we find we will always have something new to understand or another skill to master.
Lisa Michaels

Something unexpected happened on the way to writing this chapter. I thought I had a plan and soon discovered that Spirit had a different plan. I made an agreement to write about my many home-related experiences as a Natural Rhythms Facilitator, Feng Shui Consultant, Intuitive Interior Decorator, and Furniture/Window Fashion Trainer. I have collected a treasure trove of stories and elemental tips over the years and I thought I had come to a place where it was time to share them. I soon discovered that the Elements were weaving the chapter for me. They were showing me, by way of my personal home experiences, what they wanted you to experience. It is my hope that through my telling of the story you will begin to understand the POWER the Elemental Forces pack and how they play a role in our everyday life experience.

If I have learned anything over the years, it is the truth behind the saying when the student is ready, the teacher will appear. I have come to know that teachers show up in every guise imaginable. In this case, the Elements were guiding my every step, bringing me new insights. I also know when resistance shows up, and I am getting in my own way, that there is likely a breakthrough on the horizon. Then there is someone or something that brings me back to reality. As much as I want to do it my way, I am able to see there is another way that very well could be a better way. I have so much to say about reading the energy of a home or office that I thought writing about it would be easy. The deeper I listened, the more I realized the Elements wanted me to share the story right in front of me. The fear, that perhaps you too have pushed up against in the back of your mind. Or, maybe you have had a down right or even up close struggle with at some point. It is the *fear of being homeless*! Suddenly, my story went from a warm and cozy place to a whole other place, one I had no desire to visit. Yet, there it was right in front of me.

Synchronicity: the coming together of inner and outer events in a way that can't be explained by cause and effect and that is meaningful to the observer.
Trish & Rob MacGregor

It was Sunday of Labor Day weekend, 2010. I turned on the TV and caught a reality show on the *Green2* channel. I thought, *"Green,* it has to be good." My *Green* experience morphed from a three hour show into a three month life-altering drama.

Five famous and rich British people agreed to live on the streets of London with the Homeless for 10 days. They were not permitted to take any food or money with them and were given suitable clothing to wear. After all, they needed to look the part. It was quite the shock to them. One man only lasted a couple nights and after collecting enough tips from tourists for taking their photos, he bought himself a warm breakfast and then called his wife saying, "Honey, I am coming home."

I soon realized I was facing my own FEAR! I've never been on such a ride. There I was being witness to a whole other show overlaid on the TV show that I was watching. I will say, it was a pretty trippy experience, where the elements of Earth, Air, Fire, Water, and Spirit were telling their story and nobody on the show was saying a word about it. Each element came to life right there in my living room in full Technicolor for me to see, hear, and of course, feel. There was such a complexity of my own fear, the fear of those who agreed to play the part, and the fear of those who were living the life of being homeless. For those of you who understand archetypes, my role of rescuer went into overdrive. Being an empath, I was sent even deeper into feeling the collective fear of homelessness. The emotions that rapidly ran through my body were stuck in my head among thoughts too hard to bear.

It became clear to me that this was one vehicle I needed to ride in before I could honestly articulate a true expression of a *Home with Soul.* In the midst of physical pain becoming stronger and stronger in my head, I thought I was having a stroke. I had to make a decision to stop this foolishness or decide how far I would choose to ride this painful roller coaster! Could I look at my own fear and come out on the other side without taking my body into a full blown hospital experience? I took a few seconds to figure out my options. I could call a friend, the girls next door, or 911. When I listen to what my body is telling me I can avoid any manner of physical set-backs. The only thing I knew to do was to continue communicating with the elements in the best way I know how. I felt like a detective as I went on a discovery of what Spirit was telling me about the homeless world. How could I ease the pain of what I had just witnessed? What could I do to see my way out? What could I possibly do to help others see their way out of despair? What on earth (pun intended) made me tune into this? It was so profound to be in a place of such horrific pain laced with fear. In the midst of this, I was able to trust myself, my inner guidance, and the elements, all at the same time. I went into my bedroom and began a healing meditation I had learned years ago. It began to morph itself into a new elemental version. I sat with it and was amazed at the level of clarity I received from each element. Every element came forward with its story in relationship to my pain and what its teaching was for me or for the collective around homelessness.

> *We receive a powerful gift when we learn from the forces of nature.*
> *Lisa Michaels*

Message from *Earth*:

We are to honor and be in celebration of the home we have. We are a global village and our ancestors who came before us now stand behind us as they give us guidance and support to keep our planet healthy and safe for all to enjoy. We borrow Mother Earth from our children.
(Earth had more to say later.)

Message from *Air:*
Pray for those less fortunate. Holding the prayer field for those who cannot do so for themselves is vital to lifting the energy of the planet. My personal message was to share my experience through the *Power of Perspective* and the written word.

Message from *Fire*:

Letting Go (of fear) will lead to transformation. My personal message was one of taking *action* and be willing to *move* when necessary. More about this later—as I soon discovered I would be moving into a new home. *It is Passion for Life Force that has kept Home Fires burning since the beginning of time.*

Message from **Water**:
Being *Clear, Clean, and Current* with our emotional state of mind and personal feelings gives us the capacity to easily flow within our life aquarium. Surrender to the cleansing power of crying in relationship to others and to myself. Those who know me will get this. It is ok for me to cry. Once *Emotional Maturity* understands the *Power of Love* . . . a home is a natural part of life's *Ebb and Flow*. The first place we knew LOVE was within the waters of our Mother's womb prior to birth, and we long for this place of safety and comfort.

Message from **Spirit**:
It is within the *Power of Choice* that we fill the gap of *who* we are (in life) with *where* we choose to live. When Spirit is called on, our homes become a reflection of our true essence.

> *The elements are active teachers of consciousness.*
> Lisa Michaels

As I closed the meditation I heard, "*You are safe where you are, God IS, and all is well.*" I felt a pop in my head and 80% of the pain subsided. Allowing myself to let my emotional waters do their job of cleansing, I continued to talk to the Elements. Through blurred vision I picked one elemental card. It was the *Power to Stand on your Own*, **Earth** card.

Of course, that was the element I needed to hear more from. It is a basic necessity for anyone to have a home. Careers, jobs, stability, and a willingness to do what it takes to keep a roof over our heads comes from an *inner* Power. Many of the homeless have hidden or all together lost their personal power. It is not uncommon for it to be given over to alcohol and/ or drugs. Many even misuse their power through prostitution to survive. All of this leads to a crumbling of the life structure they once had. **Earth** honors *Body Wisdom* with its rhythm and cycles and yearns for humanity to reclaim its natural balance with nature.

Just days later, still in the midst pondering on what HOME means to me, I received a call from my landlord. I flipped open my phone and knew he was about to ask me to move. Later, I realized the universe had been giving me signs that this was on the way. His wife wanted a divorce and he needed his house back. Once I got over the shock, the search for a new home began. One day, my rental agent and I drove past five homes and I would not even get out of my car. The energy of the neighborhoods was not a place I would call home. I was beside myself, as I quickly discovered how the market had put a whole new spin on property values in comparison to what I could afford. I have rented a number of times since my divorce and I know what works for me and what does not work for me in my personal space. Once again, I found myself working with the elements to bring me my next home.

I worked with the Elemental Forces of Creation Oracle[3] cards almost daily to hone in on where I was emotionally and where my home beacon was leading me. I began balancing the task of packing with the task of looking, and laughed as I told friends and co-workers I was working on my P&L (packing/looking) statement all weekend. Which in itself is true: moving costs money, which I did not have planned in my budget. I was leaving a house with a beautiful yard and amazing trees, so that was what I wanted, a house with a yard. It soon became very clear that I needed to make some compromises along the way to a new home. I was bound and determined to have at least one tree that I could enjoy from my living space. I was clear that the Elements would support me in this.

As the days were flying, a friend suggested a condo, and I finally gave in. Of course, I always pay attention to signs. What happens on the way to the appointment is always key, which was a valuable lesson from my Feng Shui Master. I always tell my clients to be clear about what you ask for. That *IS* what will show up.

The first sign was that it had a couple trees that I could view from the living room. I asked for trees, and got them. I asked for an updated kitchen, and got it. I asked for clean, and got that, too. I asked to move from Ohio back to Kentucky, and got that as well. I asked for a larger bedroom, and I am happy there as well.

My brother in—law, asked me why I always seemed to live in a home with steps. That was an easy answer. Each step is a prayer of gratitude that I *can* go up and down the steps. He smiled and said, "Got it." You see, there was a time where that would not have been an easy task for me. The condo had 39 steps. Next time, there will be a limit on the number of steps. Spirit gives us what we ask for and she fills in the blanks. Once the move was over, I learned that I had no hot water in either bathtub. And neither the washer/dryer nor the furnace were working.

The furnace was on the roof and I was concerned that the crane needed to replace the furnace could break off many of my tree's branches. I quickly hugged the tree, called in the elements, and explained what was about to happen. I asked that Water move through the limbs and branches making it possible for them to bend as needed. I also asked Air to take part in moving the branches as needed. The crane driver said he had never witnessed such a thing before. Only one small branch fell to the ground, and he usually has many that break and fall.

Within weeks of moving in, I had water leaks from the roof coming through the living room ceiling. As I pondered this, I knew there was a connection to my emotional realm. I was so exhausted from the whole ordeal of moving, yet I would not allow myself to have a good old cry over the fact that I had been forced to move. Letting the emotion stay bottled up was horrible. I was in fear, and I thought if I started to cry I would go into a meltdown and probably would not be able to stop crying. I had not moved through the energy of being in a *forced* move rather moving on my own timeline. And if I didn't get the lesson it will show up again. My next move will be on my terms and I will remain clear, clean, and current with my emotions.

Four months later, I realized I had no water. The bill was paid, the neighbors had water, but I did not. It was nearly midnight when the water company came and turned my water back on telling me it was a *mystery* as to why it was off. Well, it was no mystery to me, as I knew Water was once again communicating. Our homes are a reflection of what goes on inside ourselves. I had shut off my emotions so I could cope.

I was to attend a funeral the next day that was reminding of my dad's funeral a year before. I was also in the midst of downsizing with my employer. All the phone calls and emotions had caught up with me, and I shut down as a way to cope with all the emotions: mine and many co-workers. No wonder I had no water: my home was showing me that I needed to nourish myself before I could be of any help to anyone.

I found two magazine photos of water faucets, one with water *off* and one with water *on*. I pasted them in my co-creation journal and asked Water what I was to learn from this experience. Lessons from my Water journey: I was closed off, disconnected from feeling, out of the flow, and unable to receive. How many opportunities would I *turn off* before the flow and magic begins? With Water *on* again, I am in the flow with the magic of emotions and feelings. Water *IS* life. When I am nourished I receive the flow of LOVE. Life's abundance *IS* mine. When in the flow with the power of Water and infusion I can magnetize the life I desire. Thank you, sweet Water.

> *LOVE begins at home, and it is not how much we do*
> *but how much LOVE we put in that action.*
> *Mother Teresa*

I often wonder if those on the streets are disconnected from their bodies. If they are that disconnection could eventually show up in the lack of having a home. Perhaps those who are homeless came from a weak foundation. Their life experience may have created such lack of self-respect for their bodies that they no longer have a foundation to stand on. Those on the streets may no longer feel loved.

What I did notice in the eyes and actions of the homeless was a desire to help each other. Maybe somewhere, somehow, if enough of us send love to the homeless they will be able to find the emotional support to *receive* and *know* love again. I agree with the wise words that love and world peace begins or breaks down at home. I believe that *LOVE* is key to getting off the streets. Finding a place in their own hearts to love themselves, maybe for the first time in their lives, could be the first step to finding home again. Grace and inner trust could lead them home. Perhaps even love extended from a fellow homeless person could be the golden key that sets them free.

I am also reminded of something I learned from Gregg Braden about the *power of blessing* from his book, *Secrets of the Lost Mode of Prayer*[4] and his *Modern God* CD[5]. I send a *blessing* to the homeless, a *blessing* to the circumstances that brought them to the place of no home, and I send a *blessing* to myself and others who *witness* seeing those who are on the streets without a home.

From this place of blessing, there is no room for judgment. The template is to bless those who suffer, bless what or who has caused the suffering, and bless those who are in witness to the suffering. I know that prayer can reach them and touch them in such a way that they can once again find a path back to the warmth of a home fire burning in their own heart(h).

As I do this, my *fear* of being homeless melts away. I pray the same happens for you as you allow yourself to know that you are loved and HOME is where the heart and soul reside.

> *Be the Change, you wish to see in the world!*
> *Gandhi*

Change begins at home. As a global village, it is vital that we first build strong foundations that give attention to *soul-making* within our homes. Weaving of the soul must be deeply rooted into the physical structure we come to call our home. Every home tells a story. Within minutes, I can read if a home has a soulful foundation or not. The energy of Spirit is evident in a home where *soul-making* has been woven into its very core. Without the richness of *soul-making*, our life tapestry begins to wear thin. The homeless may have pulled soul threads from their tapestry to the point of having no shirts on their backs.

Others have found a way to re-connect with Spirit so that they co-create a new, more vibrant life tapestry filled with a deepened sense of worthiness and love. Author Neale Donald Walsch[6] moved his experience of being homeless into a place where he opened his mind and heart to the healing of his soul, and there he found *home*. He listened deeply to Spirit and co-created a life tapestry so bright that it will continue to shine God's love and light for many generations to come.

Colors, textures and shapes act as bridges that lead our attention from the material world of isolated objects into the interconnected realm of the Spirit.
Anthony Lawlor

When all of my senses become alive in a visual feast of color and texture and I am immersed in the home owner's essence, I know I am in a *home with soul*. When this experience is enhanced with aromas that take me to a place of bliss, it deepens the soulfulness that is present. That is why it is called *soul food,* because the aroma touches us at such a deep level that memories can be recalled from long ago. Within a brief moment of certain scents, one can be transported to another place and time. This is another clue that I have entered a *home with soul.*

When I see a story unfolding in a home's décor that is what I call a *soul sign* or *soul signature* which gives me a clue to the nature or true essence of the homeowner. These clues play like background music in a movie. The story can be in rhythm with harmony, love, wealth, illness, hiding, fear of loss, or total inner conflict, just to name a few. It all shows up on the inside first. Then we begin to dance with this *soul signature music* as it plays out into our physical environment.

And, there is always a relationship to the elemental world.

I have come to recognize that our yearning for home comes from a primal place deep inside us. Our first sacred home comes from the creative place inside our mothers, where we first rested within her water body. We are infused with love and safety within the waters of momma's womb. We remember this and cling to its life-giving power. Water moves our emotional realm in and out of love and fear. As we travel through the birth canal, our DNA carries us home from the no-where to the now-here. Our soul continues its search for home with unremembered memories from lifetime to lifetime.

Just as tree roots go deep into Mother Earth, so do our home-roots. That first ebb & flow of birthing guides our inner instincts to find a place of safety and comfort. A baby's first cry is a plea of *"take me home."* One of the first things we do for this tiny sacred baby is to honor our new family member with a name.

Choosing a name is one of the first steps in creating a relationship with our children. I have noticed that many people I have worked with have given great thought to naming their cars and boats. However, it has never occurred to them that the relationship with their home is just as important. Blessing the sacred container we call home with a name is an example of *soul-making* and is vital to creating a relationship with our home. Regardless of where you choose to live, blessing your home with a name is a way to give gratitude for the shelter it provides for you and your family. It is up to you to infuse your home with love and it will love you in return with less needed repairs.

Inviting Spirit in and the act of creating a ceremony sets the vibrational tone of a home, office, or personal space. When making a spiritual connection with our home through ceremony, it is not unlike making vows as we do in a wedding ceremony. We are creating a bond that strengthens the relationship of those who reside within its walls. A sacred vibration is created that lives within the energy of your personal space or office.

Blessing and naming your home includes the land on which it is built. I always thank Mother Earth for her part in providing a home within our global Earth village. Light a white candle, say a prayer of gratitude, and honor your home with a name. Making this a sacred family experience invokes Gandhi's *"Be the Change"*. As we do our part in healing our planet, we must first claim our divine right to make *soul-making* of the home a promise to children and families that will follow seven generations to come. During this ceremony use Air to place the conscious intention that the home is a safe place for all who enter.

> *Time stays long enough for anyone who will use it.*
> *Leonardo Da Vinci*

As I take time to sit with Spirit's Song and how she used the homeless to move me up and out of my fears, I continue to ask questions. Thanks to the deep understanding and integration of the elements of Earth, Air, Fire, Water and Spirit my adventure with the homeless gifted me with several personal gems to add to my treasure trove of intuitive designs for the home and soul.

I discovered what it means to ASK. We ask because we know that another soul knows. Someone else has walked the walk and in sharing their journey made it possible to move through life with more grace and ease. I am in deep gratitude to my many teachers, past and future.

When stuck in Water's emotion of fear (or other emotion), use another element to shift the feeling. Release and refrain from holding onto the emotions. It is ok to cry. Tears cleanse and move the energy.

I now listen and do what benefits my soul—just like I did when I ran from the barn at 6 years old. This time, it is the world of job dueling with my spiritual warrior self. I am once again running toward home for answers which I see as another synchronicity. My passion for *soul-making* as a *House Whisperer* is the bridge between the material world and my spiritual work. I pick up what life gives me and make the most of it as I co-create each day as a best experience through Spirit's power of choice. Earth reminds me I have the power to stand on my own. Thanks to a sweet friend, I chant my new mantra: It's time! I am ready! I can do it! The discovery of what home means to me is honoring of my essence.

Hopefully, you will agree as you look around your home or office and see your *soul's signature* as it is reflected in the color, texture, style, and story you live. May you honor the *soul signs* in your home and every home that you visit. Home is sacred to each of us. Every home matters, every heart matters and every story matters. My prayer for you, your home and our planet is one of Peace and Love that is free of homelessness. And so it is.

About Paula York

Paula brings meaning to being a *House Whisperer* through her unique understanding of a physical space and how it relates to the inner soul space. Her deep intuitive skills bring clarity and insight to her Interior Creations for the Home and Soul. She gently guides people through a discovery of what their home has to say and how it is connected to their relationships, emotions, mental, and financial worlds. These discoveries often bring more balance and harmony into everyday life experiences. She shares many gifts through her healing work as a Creation Life Coach, Motivational Speaker, and *Natural Rhythms* Facilitator in northern Kentucky and Cincinnati,

Ohio. Paula can be reached at 859-653-7298 or p.york@hotmail.com http://www.thehousewhisperinglady.com/.

Chapter 10

Deepen Your Self-Love and Get Energized with Body Awareness

Leslie Clayton

It happened for me in one simple breath. At one of my first Pilates Teacher Training workshops, I rolled off the cylindrical foam roller for the first time and landed on my mat. My body melted into a relaxation unlike anything I'd ever felt before. I began to notice subtle sensations moving through me. Some felt like pulsations moving through my blood. Some were like waves of warm water washing over my body. I remember liking the feeling. Nothing else mattered in that moment. The whole world disappeared and I was the world, all at the same time. This was something very new for me, and it was my little secret at first. Not because I didn't want to tell others about it, but rather because I didn't know how to describe the feeling and I really didn't know if anyone else would care. I had been teaching Pilates for about a year by that time, so I told a few clients about my secret and attempted to guide them into this mysterious yummy surrender. Sometimes it worked for them. Sometimes it didn't. It was like an itch that I couldn't quite scratch. "Wow," I thought. "If everyone felt this, there would be no war. People would be laughing and smiling at each other ALL THE TIME!" I found peace on earth. I began a long search for more dependable ways to guide others through breath and movement that would leave them feeling whole.

I had entered the Pilates world after many years of a career in ballet and modern dance. It was fun for me to discover new ways to experience my body through Pilates, Feldenkrais, yoga, and various other forms of dance and exercise. I was secretly looking for more sweet surrender and tingling sensations. There's nothing like the first time it happens. Maybe you've had one of those experiences?

I loved introducing new people to this wonderful stuff. I consciously asked God to guide my process as I began to develop a small business called Body Awareness. I specialized in Pilates and hands-on healing modalities. It was important to me that my business help people connect to the body and feel more alive. Even if no one else knew about the treasure I had found, I was determined to plant some "yummy seeds" so others could feel this beautiful heart-centered experience. I trusted those seeds would grow in time. Occasionally, I would have the great pleasure of laughing and smiling with someone who had entered the realm of yumminess with me.

Besides being the name of my business, body awareness is a term that defines the pathway toward self-acceptance and true love. The action steps that take you on the journey inward and onto that pathway are simple, but they can be hard to choose. They require aligning your physical body with Earth and Heaven, being willing to feel your emotions fully even when it hurts, focusing your thoughts with pure intentions, and consciously choosing when to take action and when to wait for life to unfold naturally. You were born with all of this information available to you, but it takes focus and technique to put the knowledge to transformative use.

The body is alive with Earth, Water, Air and Fire. Spirit moves through the physical form any time you choose to pause and witness the breath and the dance of energy moving inside and around you. I have come to know that every body has a beautiful story to tell. The body is alive and ever changing, just as you and Nature are alive and changing in every moment. Your journey toward loving yourself is unique. If you pause and listen to your body right now, you might find that you're already doing it.

For years, I diligently shared subtle energy exercises with my clients. At first, there were some who didn't understand my interpretation of Pilates and body awareness. They were tough nuts to crack. It took me years to learn that not everyone has the same way of entering this secret inner realm. Not everyone wants to enter. I had to learn how to listen to the different kinds of bodies and personalities, and then make choices about how to introduce the gifts of this deeper, elemental body awareness.

The tough ones wanted to "work out" to lose weight or feel the burn. They were more interested in the outer, physical world appearance of their body. In order for me to connect with those people, I had to learn to deepen my own experience with the elements to help them push with intensity while maintaining the mindfulness of body awareness. As I studied the elements, I learned that the elements are teachers for body awareness. Water governs our peace and emotions, Air speaks to us about the mental realm of our concepts and beliefs, Earth houses body wisdom, and Fire is a powerful tool for transformation. We can't have change without it. It is an important alchemical ingredient that changes the matter of our physical bodies. For clients focused on working out, I used the more dynamic exercises to build intensity (Fire), which then made it much easier for them calm their minds (Air), and to merge into the inner realms to relax (Water) and hear their body wisdom (Earth).

People have different needs at different times. These distinctions took some time to uncover as well. But as my knowledge of the elements integrated into my own life, I began practicing them naturally with clients, and became aware that it is important to have enough tools to adjust a fitness ritual to match the current state of being.

For example, I have a client, Lee Anne, who exercises with us twice a week. She is a high-powered businesswoman with two children. At the time of this story, she was going through a difficult divorce. Her husband was fighting her for the company they owned together, and the legal battle ate up a lot of her real estate and assets. I was impressed with how hard she worked to maintain her certainty and self-esteem during that roller coaster ride.

Every time she showed up for her session, I would ask her, "How's your body doing today?" I knew that our bodies are in "present time." My role was to guide her out of her head and into her body. Sometimes, the pressure of the day was more than her mind and emotions could bear. Since we were not together for talk therapy, we chose to use those sessions to move energy through her body so that she could find balance again.

Sometimes we would start with a dynamic physical exercise that would push the anger and rage up and out. Sometimes her body needed a soft relaxing start. Another time we chose to do a full hour of power breathing.

This process called on the Air and Fire elements to cleanse her mind, her emotions, and balance her body. Each time, we listened deeply to Lee Anne's body and asked what she needed next. It's been a few years since that roller coaster ride, and Lee Anne is doing really well. We continue to ride the waves of life together as she uses the Body Awareness systems to find balance and stay physically fit.

It gives me so much joy when I can guide a person into her body and empower her to hear her own inner body wisdom. The body is communicating all the time. There are some simple ways to tune in and listen to it. Before I offer you specific techniques to try yourself, a few more examples may demonstrate the value of deep listening to refine body awareness.

My friend Rachel is a young woman in her 20's who is absolutely new to the idea of body awareness. She is open and curious about this mysterious realm. Her father is a medical doctor and she has always used allopathic medicine to treat her illnesses and body concerns. She has heard me and other Body Awareness instructors and clients talk about our own life-changing experiences through listening to our bodies, exercising, or meditating. She recently told me that she didn't think she could listen to her body. It almost sounded like she didn't think she was capable. The truth is, she listens to her body all the time. She just hasn't learned how to interpret what she's hearing.

I told her that from my experience of her, she was in constant dialogue with her body. My observation was that she was mostly struggling with it. Many of her complaints indicated different kinds of mid-section dis-ease (unease): upset stomach, nausea, difficulty digesting food, shortness of breath, headaches, and itchy skin. She experienced one or more of these issues randomly throughout the week. I asked her if she would like to take just a minute or so to check in with that inner realm, and I would help her interpret the news that she brought back. She bravely said, "Yes." We both took a pause. We closed our eyes to go inward. I asked her to feel her feet on the ground and then take a soft gentle breath. I asked her to scan her body and tell me what she noticed first. She noticed that it was difficult to get a full breath. Because breath is associated with the Air element and influences our mind, I asked her how she would describe her mental state of being. She said it was very busy in there. She had a lot of chaotic thoughts, songs, and memories playing around in there nonstop. She said if she closed her eyes for too long, she would begin to see monsters. She reported this was true for as many years as she can remember.

The area of her body that she pointed to was the diaphragm, which is located in the center of the body where the base of the rib cage separates the lower body from the upper body. This area, the third chakra, houses our beliefs and how we use our willpower in the world. I asked her if she wanted to go a little deeper into that place inside her. She again bravely said, "Yes." I chose to investigate the beliefs programmed into her body/mind. I asked her to finish a few statements for me.

1. The world is a _____ place to be. Her answer, "horrible"
2. People are _____. Her answer, "horrible"
3. My dad would describe me as _____. "sweet, dependable, good, hard-working, thick-skinned"
4. My mom would say _____ about me. "she is me, I am her, vicious, sweet and sour"
5. Life is _____. "ever-changing"

Rachel began to see that some of these unconscious beliefs were holding her body and her mind in a state of contraction and fear. With each realization, I could see a light twinkle in her eyes. She was beginning to recognize that there is another level of awareness just below the surface of the physical body. Before we took a break from that impromptu session, I gave Rachel a few simple breathing exercises for a daily awareness practice. We agreed to get together again soon to discover more about her inner realms and transform those discomforts.

Rachel remembered to use the breathing exercises whenever she noticed her body holding tension. Because Rachel is employed in my office, I was able to witness her pausing and taking a moment to center herself and breathe when there were too many work demands that needed attention all at the same time.

A few weeks later, we had our next private session. Rachel's body was giving us different information. On this day, she reported having felt frustrated for several days over lower back pain and stiffness. We asked her body where to begin. We checked in with her emotions, her mind, and her body to decide what actions to take. Besides her frustration with this discomfort, she didn't feel any emotional connection to this issue. Her mind seemed calm and open. So we started her journey into the Earth realm of her physical body. I asked her to lie down on the ground. She made a conscious connection to the Earth underneath her. I asked her to take a journey by slowly breathing into each body part, starting with her feet and moving toward her head. We paused with each new body part and allowed the breath to wander into those areas. When we arrived at the lower back area, I noticed that Rachel started to hold her breath. She was feeling an emotion. She noticed a tension from her lower abdomen to her chest. The whole area was trying to tell her something. I remembered that lower back pain can relate to a feeling of lack of support in life. This area of the body also houses the second chakra. Second chakra issues can indicate a wide range of scenarios, from lack of money or creativity, to giving too much of your creative energy away, to low sex drive, or unhealthy energy connections with others. In most cases it indicates lack of something, or an energy depletion of some kind.

I asked Rachel if she felt supported in her life. She said, "Yes." She noticed that since our last meeting she had been feeling much better with regard to feeling safe in the world. I asked her to describe where she felt the most support and then the least amount of support. As she explored the contrast of those two ideas, she started to feel her emotions again. The issue of responsibility with her closest friends began to emerge. She was feeling sad about a loss of connection with a few of her best girlfriends. She was feeling irresponsible about not being more available for them as they were going through major life changes. She had pulled away from her sweet friends because she didn't understand some of their personal choices, and she felt frustrated and upset about their decisions. She cared so much about their future happiness that it caused her physical pain to see that their choices could bring them unhappiness.

This made sense to me because I looked at Rachel's natal chart before that session. A natal chart is a simple yet complex chart that shows where the sun, moon, stars, and planets were at the time of your birth. Each of these celestial bodies carries volumes of information and provides dynamic energy that influences our human experience.

Rachel's natal chart shows that she was born with a lot of Water in her energetic life design. Water is our greatest teacher of love. Watery people tend to feel or empathize with others and they tend to merge their feelings with others. It can be hard for them to determine if they are feeling their own feelings or someone else's. Rachel happens to have strong Waters that are like the love that a mother and father have for their children, and also the kind of Water that asks you to dive deep into the darkest unknown areas of your emotional body. Most people with this mixture of Water will tell you that they are intensely emotional at times; experiencing their feelings can seem like a life and death experience. The value of this kind of Water is that it can teach you about trusting life and love beyond your ego's fear and need to control every situation. When you learn to surrender to love, your life is transformed.

Rachel's willingness to dive deep into her feeling Waters and to open her mind made it easy for her to use the next set of exercises to shift the energy connections that were tying up her emotions. First, she identified her individual friends. Next, she consciously cleared the energy connections between her and them. Finally, and with God's assistance, she forgave herself and her friends for each issue that came into her awareness during the session. She was feeling much lighter emotionally. After she felt complete with the energy clearing exercises, she drew five elemental cards from the Natural Rhythms oracle deck. She was able to hear the message with new ears as she put the cards in front of her.

Spirit said, "Grace & Trust." Water said, "Nourishment." Air said, "Ethereal Allies." Fire said, "Warmth." Earth said, "Body Wisdom."

She interpreted the oracle cards for herself. "Begin to trust in the world, and take any challenges or difficulties with grace. Accept what the world has in store for you. It will nourish your body instead of depleting it. I have felt my Ethereal Allies aligning with me more than ever. Before, I knew they were there, but now I **feel** that they are there to guide and assist me."

We completed the session with physical exercises that would open the muscles and energy pathways of her lower back. I used some muscle energy techniques with resistance stretching for her hamstrings. Then I showed her a Pilates hamstring exercise on the Wunda Chair that she could do every day, whenever she felt her back stiffen up. She felt much better and seemed empowered to have learned some new ways to listen and interpret how her body talks to her.

Rachel's story is a beautiful example of how life isn't always roses and daffodils. The body may have some dark or shadowy caves inside. It's a little scary for some people to venture into this inner realm. If you feel a little fearful about looking inside, I recommend finding a trained coach to guide you through some safe easy steps. Find someone to hold your hand as you take that journey.

The value of deepening your awareness of the inner terrain is priceless. It's a doorway toward living a life filled with happiness and freedom. As you get better at connecting and listening to your body wisdom, it is easier to make choices that support your health and wellness. Do you love yourself enough to learn more about your inner world?

I've mapped out a simple five-step process that will only take two minutes, and will help you develop greater awareness of your body wisdom.

1. The first step is easy. Decide that you want to feel connected and aligned with your life. State your intention aloud or in writing.

2. In this step, say "hello" to your body. Have a seat or lie down. Align your body so that your spine is relatively straight or neutral. Take a breath and feel the air pass through your nose and into your lungs. Then feel the breath leave your body. Notice the rise and fall of the breath in your body. Relax and repeat. Notice how your body enjoys the breath.

3. Next, start moving your body like you're yawning and if you begin to yawn, go all the way into it. Try to identify where your body feels the stretch. Is there any noticeable stiffness in your body?

4. Now come back to your original starting position and notice your body again. Continue to breathe very naturally, softly. Notice any changes, pulsations, or sensations. Become aware of your state of being. You may feel physical sensations like relaxation, hunger, or cold. You might become aware of an emotional sensation like frustration, excitement, or happiness. You may notice that you are

having a difficult time focusing on the body. Your mind might be very active and pulling your attention away from the exercise. Anything you notice is perfect.

5. Ask your body if there is anything it needs to feel more balanced and at peace. Wait for an answer. Trust that the answer you hear is an important message. It helps to write down your message. Your mind moves really fast and sometimes the message gets lost if you don't write it down. As you practice this, you will develop certainty, and it will be easier to hear the message and apply it to your life.

As you take the first few steps in the exercises above, scan your body to identify any sensations. These can be subtle like your heart beating, blood moving, or more dynamic like muscle stiffness or discomforts. Everyone has the ability to become aware of these sensations. If you don't notice anything yet, take another breath and relax. Keep following your breath as it moves into and out of your nose. Notice the rise and fall of your lungs as you breathe. Keep this as soft and gentle as possible.

Let's say you're noticing that your body is tired and your energy level is low. This could be caused by a number of different reasons, from nutritional deficiencies to lack of sleep or an illness that has wiped out your energy level. Has this been a recurring problem or an every-once-in-a-while issue? Ask your body what it needs to reboot your systems. You might hear, feel, or just know the answer.

The elements of Earth, Water, Air, and Fire are moving through our bodies like rivers, waves, and/or energy currents. When these energies are in balance and moving freely, that blissful yummy feeling is there, too. Spirit is dancing between and through the elements to unite us in oneness.

Your body is the doorway into your wholeness. As you begin to trust your body's wisdom, and you respond to that wisdom with techniques that help the body release and align, life becomes more fun and easier. You don't have to travel the globe or seek out gurus to become enlightened. You have everything within you.

You are a unique human being who experiences life through your very own perspective. As you develop a deeper communication and connection to how your body processes those experiences, you can enhance your connection to life. The fun begins as you start to ask your body a few simple questions, interpret your answers, and make new choices that will shift challenging ideas or release feelings and inspire you to energize your life.

Choose one of these energy exercises as another option for improving your current state of being.

1. Go outside and take a brisk walk.
2. Put your favorite music on and move your body randomly around the room. Some people call this "DANCING."
3. If you know a little yoga, do the sun salutation.
4. If you know a little Pilates, do the basic 10 mat exercises.
5. Take 10 to 50 full, powerful breaths.

The best medicine for depletion is to add more energy. All of these exercises add energy by using the unified field of elements, and they will shift your state of being. Remember, if you are depleted because of an illness, you will need to take it slow and gradually build the energy. Too much Fire can overwhelm your system and deplete you further.

I'll tell you a story about a couple in their 60's who come to Body Awareness on Monday mornings at 8:00. Diane and Lee have been doing Pilates with me for several years now. They are both committed to staying in shape as they age and they are dedicated to staying on a regular exercise schedule. One morning they both dragged their bodies into the studio. They were a little less enthusiastic than usual. They'd had a very full weekend with their families, including parties and dinners with their children and grandchildren. They almost cancelled their session, but chose to honor our commitment. They didn't want to leave me with an open hour on my schedule. None of us went into this session expecting miracles. We simply began our series of warm-ups as usual. I didn't want to push their bodies too hard this morning so we very gradually built the intensity of the session, finishing with some standing stretches. After the session, Diane said, "Ya know, I feel better!" Lee said, "Yeah, me too." They both found that their bodies and their minds were ready to move out into their Monday morning with full energy levels restored.

Just Do It! The Fire realm is about action. Without it, nothing changes. Fire cannot do its work without a blend of Earth, Water, Air, and Spirit to guide and transform the situation at hand. When we add consciousness to our action choices, the transformation is more satisfying.

If you choose to perform a few energy exercises, and afterwards you don't feel a change in your energy level, ask your body what it needs more of. Maybe you will need to add some high-energy food to your daily diet. Filling your body with foods rich with phytonutrients and the right balance of vitamins and minerals will enhance your energy levels. Sometimes, you might simply need more sleep.

There are some people who feel too much energy in their bodies. They have the feeling that they are going to jump out of their skin or need to run a marathon. This fiery energy can make life uncomfortable. Don't be fooled. Too much energy can be just as difficult a problem as depleted energy. An excess of disharmonious or unsettled energy can make it hard for your body to completely relax into a state of flexible balance or homeostasis.

I have a client who is in the process of learning to teach Pilates. He is a 33-year-old athlete who has discovered that many years of pushing the body too hard will burn you out. Imagine how too much heat on the stove or the grill will burn the life out of your food. Jack was a world-class athlete preparing for the 2004 Olympic games in track and field. He realized that path was not going to fulfill his life purpose. He shifted his focus toward business and to being in service to others while using his natural talents in sports and fitness. He enjoys studying diverse techniques, from swimming to martial arts, yoga to power lifting. Recently he had to shift his exercise intensity because of some acid reflux and excessive tension in his neck and shoulders. Pilates brings a softer kind of strength to his body. He can focus on building core strength without burning himself out physically.

As I listened to Jack's story, I heard clues about which elements are strong in him. He is a voracious reader and loves to learn new ideas and skills. These qualities are related to the Air realm. He likes to keep moving from one project to the next. This is a Fire energy trait. He knows how to take his time and be present with others even while he is very busy. This trait shares both Earth and Water qualities. He is calm and peaceful on the outside, while his mind is racing with creative ideas on the inside. These Air realm thoughts and ideas generate intense Fire energy in Jack's body. If he doesn't find a way to move the energy, the pressure builds, creating conflicts, and leaving him feeling out of balance with life.

As a natural athlete, Jack spent years pushing his body to maximum performance in sports. This was a perfect way for him to move the Fire energy until his body started having physical issues that require a more restorative approach. Jack is working on balancing his body, mind, and spirit by choosing forms of exercise that offer intensity when he needs it, like basketball, biking or Kettlebells, and new gentle tools for body restoration. He uses his intuition to listen and discover what his body needs next. He uses body awareness to navigate the journey through his adventurous life.

Many athletes have a strong regime that leaves no room for deviation. On one hand, I can appreciate that. Without that discipline and dedication, an athlete cannot meet goals or win the gold. For an athlete, or anyone creating a rich and fulfilling life, the true talent is learning how to work while also listening to the body. That's how to know when it's time to rest and when it's time to push for the next level of excellence.

When you check in with your current state of being, there is always more going on than appears on the surface. Remember that it can take a moment to surrender deeply into your body. First do the five-step process explained earlier.

There are infinite possibilities for these states of being. Learning to listen and apply movement to celebrate, energize, and clear disharmonious energy in the body is what it's all about. If you take the five-step process, apply some movement and you still feel a disharmonious energy, look for a Natural Rhythms Creational Life Coach to help you follow the clues, unravel the mystery, and support you in taking your personal process to the next level.

Some say that "We teach best what we need to learn." My personal experiences led me directly to the teaching I have shared with you. Would you believe me if I told you that I, a body awareness instructor, spent most of my life disconnected from my body and afraid to move? I spent years simply physically showing up to where I was supposed to be. I studied ballet and went on to have a beautiful dance career quietly navigating what I thought would be the safest route to get through life. But I was not having any fun.

I remember the first time a healer told me that I wasn't "in my body." That phrase did not make sense to me. I heard it several times, and from different people, before I began to understand the meaning and their concern. I learned that many people who experience trauma will compensate by living just outside their physical body. One way of defining this state of being is to say someone is unconscious because of subconscious issues. These patterns of unconsciousness run deep throughout humanity. Symptoms can look like people having difficulty with relationships, illnesses, addictions, confusion, lack of focus, and more.

When I was very young, there were a few events that startled me. I must have held my breath and jumped out of my body just a little bit each time. I didn't know how to ask for help and I didn't realize help was needed. I had a few shocking sexual experiences at different ages of development that confused me. From my little girl eyes and ears, the world was scary and not safe. Each time, I created beliefs that I was wrong and stupid, and these compounded and seemed real. Fear kept me tight on the inside and disconnected from my sweet little body. You name it, I was afraid of it. Every projection that I made about other people being mean and harsh or life being scary created an emotional disconnection in me. I can remember being in tremendous pain while I was with the family and friends I loved.

The heaviness of not feeling love in my life made it hard to smile. I experienced years of depression, which made it difficult for me to move my body, but my body came naturally equipped with a talent for dance. If my ballet teacher hadn't told my mother and me about those talents when I was around eight, I might not have known to keep dancing.

I struggled with work and personal relationships until I consciously asked God to assist me. Almost immediately I noticed things shifting. I randomly stopped at a bookstore and a few books found me. I was invited to two life-changing workshops, one called *Essence of Being* and the other called *Radical Forgiveness* that helped me trust my heart and feel love in a very new way. I learned to forgive myself for the ways that I abused my body and devalued myself. I paid close attention as my consciousness was being raised up to new levels of compassion for myself and others. My love-hate relationship with my body and dance was transformed into gratitude, appreciation sprinkled with loving acceptance. I was beginning to have a romance with life. It took years of practice and gentle support from others to shift my fearful experiences to ones filled with safety, freedom, happiness, and LOVE.

I remember the day that I woke up and realized "I'm happy." I asked myself, "When did that happen?" I felt happy just driving down the road. I started humming and singing again. I scanned my recent days and months to identify the source of this happiness. Was it about money, my relationships, my business successes? I wasn't sure at first. I didn't have much money, my relationships were much better than before, however I still had some on-and-off tension and power struggles. My business was good, yet always kept me pushing for the next deadline. I had almost no down time. Where did this happy state come from? It came on gradually, so it was hard to identify the shift.

The many layers of my struggle were opened up and the unconscious patterns unraveled with journaling, breath work, prayer, dance, and new, focused intentions. I began to use dancing and meditating as a form of prayer, although many of the tools I used are considered to be metaphysical, or beyond physical. The human energy field consists of several vibrational layers of light. The chakra system is among these layers and is connected to the spinal column. The other layers are interconnected egg-shaped auras that carry every memory, thought, belief, illness, and pure love. This unseen realm has carbon copies of the physical world inside it. As I learned to clear and balance my chakras and release energy disturbances, my earthly body began to heal.

Accessing my body awareness gives me the courage to move forward when life gets hard. I know from experience that my body, mind, and emotions are linked together. If one is upset, it pulls the others into chaos. The chaos doesn't scare me anymore. I've made best friends of my body and the elements. I never feel alone and I'm rich with resources and choices for living with inner peace and outer aliveness. Let every day be enhanced as the elements teach you how to tend your body. The following set of exercises work together to raise your body awareness and deepen your self-love.

Body Awareness Techniques for Deeper Levels of Transformation

Aligning the Body

Become aware of your posture as you move through this gravitational world. Your posture influences your state of being. When your bones and spine are aligned properly, you will have less compression on your joints and your muscles will function with ease and grace. The energy that moves through your meridians will flow like rivers and your vital organs will receive the nutrients that they are thirsty for. Your body needs good food, clean water, exercise, and rest to thrive on this Earth. Learn to listen to your body and tend to it as a sacred temple. Love and appreciate your body, and the Earth will feel your intention. She will align with your health. Your body is directly connected to the planet. Every step you take to benefit the planet will support your own well-being.

Educating the Mind

Bring consciousness to your life. The thoughts that drive you forward are the seeds of your creations. Use your mind with focus and clear intentions toward your goals. It doesn't matter how small the task. Consciously choose the food you eat, the water you drink, the words you say to yourself and others. Your mind is the Air realm and Air fuels the Fire realm. You must become aware of your deeper thoughts and underlying beliefs and intentions. It is hard work but well worth the effort. You will begin to see and feel the benefits because you will naturally be more successful and happy in your life. If you're stuck in an unhealthy situation or are getting unwanted results, stop blaming others. Look closely at the thoughts you've held and the actions you've taken that have delivered those results. Your mind is a powerful doorway into your super-conscious higher self. Breath work, meditation, journaling, sound therapy, and coaching will help you "clear the Air." Peace lives in the Air realm. Breathe it into your heart!

134

Opening the Heart

Travel deep down into your heart center. Gently breathe unconditional love into this sacred space. Begin to stretch the corners of your mouth wide until they turn upward. Feel the sensations of this "inner smile" in your upper pallet. Now, breathe again and send that breath down into your heart with sincerity. Send love to yourself. Relax and know that you are loved.

Emotions swim on the waves of your heart's song. Dancing, singing, exercising, and connecting with your loved ones will open your heart. Have you ever seen something so beautiful that your heart hurt? That is a form of love. Animals, babies, and movies can have this effect. If you've been tight inside like I was, it might hurt a little or a lot at first. Cry. Every tear is valuable and is being shed for your highest good. Let those tears help to wash away pain and suffering. Don't hold anything back. Look into the eyes of the people in your life and receive them as blessings. When you begin to see your reflection in their eyes and you know that we are all one, you will be in your open heart. Your presence on the planet is a precious asset to humanity. The journey from your head to your heart takes practice and patience. The rewards are rich and will nourish you in ways that will delight you for a lifetime.

Activating Spirit

Pray. Invite the God of your heart to activate your spiritual light. The act of connecting with God/Goddess is prayer. Use your Fire to transform and create the unfolding story of your life. Let go as you dance with Spirit and be a loving partner to your precious life. Be gentle with life and remember you're not alone as you waltz, tango, or cha-cha. When your dance gets out of sync, return to your heart and reconnect. Own your choices with true purpose. Every choice matters.

The elements of Earth, Air, Water, Fire, and Spirit are vibrating and swirling together to create your body. Each cell in your body performs a specific task to purposefully create your physical form. Each breath you take is filled with life force energy from Spirit. You can participate in your cells' success rate by raising your consciousness and receiving love from all directions. This act of receiving is the greatest give you can give to humanity. Blessings to you.

About Leslie Clayton

Leslie is passionate about helping women find strength, balance, and beauty. With more than 30 years of dance and exercise training, she uses physical and metaphysical exercises to assist her clients with body awareness. Leslie founded the first Pilates studio in Atlanta in 1993. Body Awareness Studio is currently the Georgia host site for Balanced Body Pilates Teacher Training. Leslie combines her compassion and expertise to develop conscious Pilates instructors. Leslie is also a Creation Life Coach with Natural Rhythms Institute and is committed to guiding people into their heart to use Divine Love to transform their lives.

http://bodyawarenessstudio.com
http://balancedbody.com
http://naturalrhythms.org

Chapter 11

Simple Life Success Rx: A Daily Dose of Dance

Lisa Michaels

You've seen through the powerful stories and examples of these Natural Rhythms experts the rich and varied ways Nature's elemental forces can be used to support you in every area of life. Because they form the core of creation they can assist you with anything. How they help you will depend on your development and the realm/s in which you need guidance.

While conscious creation requires planning, making choices, releasing blocked emotions, taking action, and staying focused, there is one easy thing that you can do every day to energize your success . . . DANCE.

There's a tribal saying, "If you can move, you can dance." Dance is something we all have in common, like a heartbeat. And like a heartbeat, dance can help you come alive and activate your dreams, integrating and energizing them internally and externally.

This topic has a special place in my heart because I know the deep value dance can bring to almost any setting. I have had a lifetime devotion to dance: first as a dancer myself, then as a co-owner/director/primary teacher of a 500-pupil ballet school. And for the past 12 years, I have been working with dance as a personal development tool.

Dance is a natural expression of emotion for us all. Toddlers dance to enlivening music, dogs dance when their "peeps" come home, our hearts dance with joy, and even leaves and trees dance in the wind. Dance can be structured, certainly. Yet the most natural dance of the body is what I would call "expressive or conscious dance"—movements that are inspired from within.

Structured dance develops consciousness from the outside in. Dancers see and hear the instruction and apply it to their bodies, creating the appropriate dance shape, form, and timing. This increases the dancer's physical coordination, their patterned thinking ability, and their capacity for "harmonic synergy" (which I call the level of consciousness required to coordinate physical movement in time to the music, expanding the brain's ability to effectively function on multiple levels at one time).

Expressive/conscious dance works in the opposite direction—from the inside out. It connects to the wellspring of creativity in the inner landscape of the dancer and then brings that ability to the outer world, increasing the capacity for creative problem solving, innovation, and personal expression. I have discovered that free movement brings into the physical realm the energy of the intent on a spiritual, emotional, and intellectual level.

Expressive dance takes the dancer away from the security of knowing the steps, so it is important to create a safe environment for personal expression where any possible feelings of self-consciousness and fear of judgment are replaced by comfort with expressing their deepest feelings and essence.

If you want to free your thinking, increase your creativity, free a block in your life, or fully enliven your creations, you literally need to move in new ways. Finding new movements shifts your energy. Riding the rhythmic musical wave while dancing moves you into a trance state, allowing access to inner realms and awareness not found in your ordinary reality. Dance can be used for increasing personal expression, opening to creative insight, connecting to the Divine within, and accessing deep levels of soul transformation.

Because your body forms the container for your personal connection to all of the elements, when you rhythmically move it, with conscious intent, you are literally moving all the elemental realms at once, which activates your intention. With rhythmic movement you activate: 1) your earthen physical container, 2) your watery emotional energy, 3) your mental air realm, 4) your fiery life force, and 5) your spiritual soul essence expression. Comprising the fundamental forces—Earth, Water, Air, Fire, and Spirit—your body provides you with a portal to the core essence of creation.

Without movement and the fiery energy it creates, the physical body becomes stagnant and lacks life force. Dance provides an exceptional way to ignite your life force and generate energy. As a teacher/facilitator, this is hands-down the most potent workshop tool I use to help people clear old energies, activate their creation intentions, and integrate anything they've learned. Even though I appreciate and love many other forms of movement and lots of other facilitation tools, for me dance provides the most powerful and consistent results.

So, if you want to keep your energy clear, your success vitalized, your creations enlivened, and your feminine essence nourished, then get in a daily dose of DANCE! Honestly, it only needs to be five minutes and this Natural Rhythms life success Rx will really boost your creation power.

Additional Benefits of Conscious Dance

In conscious dance you experience your natural rhythm in harmony with the elemental forces of creation, with physical, mental, emotional, and spiritual benefits.

Physical: Regular participation in conscious dance produces an improved heart rate, better circulation, increased energy, and respiratory health. It leads to weight loss and reduced stress. Improved flexibility, stamina, and balance are also benefits to conscious dance done regularly.

Mental and Emotional: Conscious dance challenges us to use our brains differently. New channels of thought and perspective open. Conscious dance unblocks stagnant emotional energy. Unacknowledged rage and sadness—as well as joy—can emerge during conscious dance. As you dance with intention and activation, you become free from issues you hadn't realized were affecting your thoughts, feelings, and beliefs.

Spiritual: Through conscious dance you attain a higher purpose, a connection with the Divine, an inner knowing, Oneness with the Universe, and private centeredness. Activational Dance combines intention and activation to stimulate a specific spiritual energy. Sacred Dance is a form of conscious dance in which connection to the Divine is the intent.

As you forget about your outer body and your daily routine, the act of dancing for a conscious purpose connects you with the natural rhythms and the energies of the universe and the elemental forces of creation within you. The result: freedom and joy that go far beyond the conscious dance itself.

How to Bring Conscious Dance into Your Life

Conscious dance can be done anywhere, anytime. Simply put on some music, close your eyes, breathe deeply, and let your body start moving. Consciously determine the intention of your dance. Stay focused on that intent as your body moves with the music. Through intention and activation, you will attain a heightened consciousness, a transcendental state of mental and physical unity.

Dance alone or with friends and family. Join conscious dance gatherings or classes in your community. Seek out online magazines, forums, and workshops. You are limited only by your own imagination.

Through conscious dance, you can direct the energies of your mind and enliven your creative power. The result: your life will be enriched with heightened creativity, grace, stamina, strength, accomplishment, beauty, joy, and love.

The Rhythmic Timing Dance of Creation

Working with the rhythmic timings of nature is like listening to the music when you dance. There is a certain musical point when it is most effective to begin the movement or step on to the dance floor—the count of one. The same holds true for the creational dance of your life. Certain points make the best time to take powerful and intentional steps into the flow of creation.

Both the sun and the moon have great points for stepping in. The sun makes points in a solar yearly cycle, while the lunar cycle creates a conscious entrance point each month on the new moon. The problem is, most of us have forgotten to listen to the celestial music Mother Nature plays, so that we can dance in harmony with her rhythms.

If you forgot to listen to the music during a waltz, you would never be effective or be filled with the feeling of grace. There is something magical that happens when you step in time to the music and coordinate your steps with grace and harmony. When you are in rhythm, an amazing feeling begins to flow inside which uplifts, centers, balances, and energizes you.

The same holds true as you dance with the sun, moon, and stars by aligning with celestial music in the dance of your life—more grace enters. You become better able to handle the times when the emotional waters of life may be rough, because you learn how to realign yourself and get back in sync with the flow.

In any type of dance, you learn how to do this because you practice. No matter how the previous "phrase or cycle" went, you start again. You assess how well you did, evaluate what you can adjust next time then re-center, realign, and start on count one again; practicing over and over until the flow is smooth and grace-filled.

When you discover how to hold the creation dance of your life in the same way, you are less frustrated with the outcome of any particular situation. You simply know that you need to evaluate your movements and energy, realign with the music, and begin again.

If a dancer gives up her practice in frustration and never goes back to it, she misses the magical feeling of grace that enters when the bumpy places are finally smoothed out. She will end up repeating the same inner block throughout life until she learns to move through that energy.
So, if you have tried setting intentions and focusing on creation, but feel like you haven't reached your goals or dreams yet, it is time to realign and get back in step. Grace comes from getting in the magical flow of the music and the dance, not from sitting on the side lines waiting. You actually have to be practicing the movements to find the flow.
Stepping out to the celestial music of the moon on any new moon is a wonderful and powerful entry point to energize your creations. If you are ready to practice, or it's your first time to move consciously onto the

creational dance floor of your life, you want to begin your preparations now for the next new moon. To find out about the next new moon download a free Sacred Timings Yearly Reference Guide at http://naturalrhythms.org and get your creations moving.

From the beating of your own heart drum to the rising and setting of the sun, Nature's elemental forces of creation provide the rhythmic pulse for your sacred, success-filled dance of life.

When Nature's energies and rhythms are honored as the profound teachers and guides they are, they readily bring assistance and clarity to boost your capacity to create success in your life. The more you continue to learn and grow with the elemental forces as your guides, the better able you are to move from simply striving to vitally thriving!

Natural Rhythms
A Daily Dose of Dance

Our Contribution

A portion of the proceeds from the sale of this book is donated to these global movements.

VDAY: A Global Movement to End Violence Against Women and Girls
http://www.vday.org/home

THE GIRL EFFECT, n.—The unique potential of 600 million adolescent girls to end poverty for themselves and the world.
http://www.girleffect.org/

HALF THE SKY: A movement to raise the status of women to help end global poverty.
http://www.halftheskymovement.org/

SACRED DANCE GUILD: Dancing the Sacred, Moving the World
http://www.sacreddanceguild.org/

References

Overall book editor: Kate Stockman

Chapter 1, 2, and 11: Lisa Michaels
    Editor: Kate Stockman

Chapter 3: Mackey McNeill CPA
    Editor: Jana Jopson

Chapter 4: Claudia Harsh MD
1. Harsh, C. *"Finding Grace and Balance in the Cycle of Life: Exploring Integrative Gynecology"*, iUniverse, 2010. www.graceandbalance.com
2. Life Success Seminars, P.O. Box 1369, Westchester, OH 45071 www.lifesuccessseminars.com
3. Michaels, L. www.naturalrhythms.org
4. Christine, N. www.magdalenemysteries.com
    Editor: Mary Pierce Brosmer

Chapter 5: Helen Magers LPCC
1. Bradshaw, John, *Healing the Shame That Binds You.* Deerfield Beach, Fl.: Health Communications, Inc., 1988
2. Kurtz, Ernest, *Same and Guilt. IUniverse,* Lincoln, NE, 2007
3. Lisa Michaels, *Natural Rhythms, Connect the Creational Dance of Your Life to the Pulse of the Universe*, Institute of Conscious Expression, Atlanta, GA, 2008
4. 4. Breathnach, Sarah Ban, *Simple Abundance,* Warner Books, New York, NY, 1995
5. Middleton-Moz, Jane, *Shame and Guilt: Masters of Disguise.* Health Communications, Inc. Deerfield Beach, FL, 1990.

Chapter 6: Tammy Huber-Wilkins MD

1. Marianne Williamson, *A Return To Love: Reflections on the Principles of A Course in Miracles*, Harper Collins, 1992. Section3, pages 190-191.
2. Lisa Michaels, *Natural Rhythms, Connect the Creational Dance of Your Life to the Pulse of the Universe*, Institute of Conscious Expression, 2008.
3. Marianne Williamson, *A Return To Love: Reflections on the Principles of A Course in Miracles,* Harper Collins, 1992. Section3, pages 190-191.
4. Marianne Williamson, *A Return To Love: Reflections on the Principles of A Course in Miracles*, Harper Collins, 1992. Section3, pages 190-191.
5. Life Applications Study Bible, New International Version, Tyndale House Publishers Inc, 1991.
6. Lisa Michaels, *Natural Rhythms, Connect the Creational Dance of Your Life to the Pulse of the Universe*, Institute of Conscious Expression, 2008.
7. Lisa Michaels, *Natural Rhythms, Connect the Creational Dance of Your Life to the Pulse of the Universe*, Institute of Conscious Expression, 2008, pages 207-228.
8. Marianne Williamson, *A Return To Love: Reflections on the Principles of A Course in Miracles*, Harper Collins, 1992. Section3, pages 190-191.
9. Lisa Michaels, *Natural Rhythms, Connect the Creational Dance of Your Life to the Pulse of the Universe*, Institute of Conscious Expression, 2008.

Chapter 7: Judy Keating MA

1. Derived from my learning while being trained by Martha Beck as a life coach.
2. Noah St. John *The Secret Code of Success 7 Hidden Steps to More Wealth and Happiness,* Collins Business 2009.
3. Etch A Sketch is a registered trademark for a mechanical drawing toy manufactured by the Ohio Art Company.
4. Lisa Michaels *Natural Rhythms Connect the Creational Dance of Your Life to the Pulse of the Universe* page 189, Institute of Conscious Expression Company 2008.
Editor: Teresa Kelly

Chapter 8: Chantal Debrosse
Lisa Michaels *Natural Rhythms Connect the Creational Dance of Your Life to the Pulse of the Universe,* Institute of Conscious Expression Company 2008.

Chapter 9: Paula York
1. Decorating Den Interiors: Franchise System based in Easton, Maryland
2. Green Channel offered on Cable Television
3. Lisa Michaels *Elemental Forces of Creation Oracle,* Institute of Conscious Expression, Company 2005.
4. Gregg Braden *Secrets of the Lost Mode of Prayer,* Hay House Publishing 2006.
5. Gregg Braden *Modern God* CD
6. Neale Donald Walsch Author of *Conversations with God Trilogy,* GP Putnam's Sons 1996.
   Editor: Cheryl Birch

Chapter 10: Leslie Clayton
1. Lisa Michaels, *Natural Rhythms, Connect the Creational Dance of Your Life to the Pulse of the Universe,* Institute of Conscious Expression, 2008
2. Dr. Fernand Poulin, White Winds Institute, training manual (2004) Not published
3. Dr. Randolph Stone, DC DO, *Polarity Therapy, Volume 1* (1948-1957)
   Editors: Jamie Cameron & Bonnie Sparling

About Lisa Michaels
Natural Rhythms Institute President

Celebrated elemental wisdom teacher and author, Lisa Michaels teaches you how to connect with the profound power of Nature so you can dramatically increase your ability to successfully thrive in every area of life. Recognized by Hay House Publishing as a mover and shaker, Lisa assists you in creating more personal and professional success in her products, workshops, and facilitator and coach trainings. In addition to this book, her most current products include the book *Natural Rhythms*, the *Elemental Forces of Creation Oracle,* and the *Elemental Forces of Creation Audio Book.* Lisa's work has helped thousands of people find keys to moving their lives and businesses forward by unlocking their natural growth potential.

Download your free Natural Rhythms Starter Kit today at http:// naturalrhythms.org.

http://naturalrhythms.org/

Natural Rhythms Institute Career Enhancement Training Programs

Yes, we can help you begin becoming a Natural Rhythms leader today!

Natural Rhythms Success Strategist
Learn to apply the Natural Rhythms principles to assist your clients and customers in gaining more success by aligning with the natural world. As the foundation of our career enhancement programs, this level is a prerequisite for all our additional trainings.

Natural Rhythms Creation Coach
Deepen your ability to help your clients clear energy that may be blocking their progress in every elemental realm (Earth/physical, Water/emotional, Air/mental, Fire/action, Spirit/spiritual essence) so they can successfully direct their creation energy.

Natural Rhythms Ceremonialist
Discover ways to utilize the Natural Rhythms principles in order to create beautiful and meaningful ceremonies for your community.

Natural Rhythms Certified Facilitator
Become a certified facilitator of all three levels of our licensed, proven program. This training teaches you to use accelerated learning techniques to facilitate all 15 full weekends of this successful and exciting material.

Natural Rhythms Expert
Take your Natural Rhythms experience to its full expression by becoming proficient in product development and platform building by becoming a licensed expert in your area of expertise.

The Elemental Forces of Creation Oracle

The *Elemental Forces of Creation Oracle* provides a simple yet powerful tool for instantly accessing the wisdom and guidance of the elements of Earth, Water, Air, Fire, and Spirit. This unique set of 90 full color Elemental cards, created by Lisa Michaels and illustrator Prescott Hill, comes with a 60-page manual. The oracle guides you into a living relationship with the elements. they work with you to increase your inner knowing, develop deeper self-awareness, and actively expand your life expression.

90-card Oracle Deck   ISBN 0-9715994-2-4

CPSIA information can be obtained at www.ICGtesting.com
Printed in the USA
LVOW031124270911

247970LV00002B/1/P

9 781452 537511